PENGUIN ANANDA
THE CAVE

Born and brought up in Mumbai, Alok Kejriwal is a serial digital entrepreneur and is currently the CEO and co-founder of Games2win. His first two companies, contests2win.com and Mobile2win, pioneered digital gaming and promotions in the world. Mobile2win was later acquired by the Walt Disney Co. Besides being a businessperson, Alok is also a passionate speaker and a mentor for emerging entrepreneurs. Alok has spoken at over 100 conferences, including at venues such as the Wharton School and Harvard Business School, and many of the IIMs and IITs.

Website: http://therodinhoods.com
Twitter: https://twitter.com/rodinhood
LinkedIn: https://www.linkedin.com/in/alokkejriwal/
Instagram: https://www.instagram.com/rodinhood/
Email: alok@rodinhood.com

THE
CAVE

An Internet Entrepreneur's
Spiritual Journey

ALOK
KEJRIWAL

PENGUIN
ANANDA

An imprint of Penguin Random House

PENGUIN ANANDA

USA | Canada | UK | Ireland | Australia
New Zealand | India | South Africa | China

Penguin Ananda is part of the Penguin Random House group of companies
whose addresses can be found at global.penguinrandomhouse.com

Published by Penguin Random House India Pvt. Ltd
4th Floor, Capital Tower 1, MG Road,
Gurugram 122 002, Haryana, India

Penguin
Random House
India

First published by Westland Publications Private Limited in 2020
Published in Penguin Ananda by Penguin Random House India 2022

ISBN 9780143459156

Typeset by SÜRYA, New Delhi
Printed at Replika Press Pvt. Ltd, India

www.penguin.co.in

MIX
Paper from
responsible sources
FSC® C016779

Offered at the lotus feet of:
Gurudev Sri Sri Ravi Shankar, Mahavatar Babaji &
Lord Bankey Bihari of Vrindavan

Dedicated to Chhavi, Nana, Anushka, Amaya

CONTENTS

INTRODUCTION

In November 2011, I visited a remote cave in the Himalayan mountain regions of Ranikhet in Uttarakhand, India. The cave changed me forever.

I have lived an unusual life. I was born to an affluent and young couple. My father was a textiles factory owner, and his father (my Dada) an established financier. My mother, barely nineteen, was a pampered 'bahu' (bride of the house). In the Marwari joint family that they belonged to, I was the first grandchild. My parents lived on South Mumbai's posh Nepean Sea Road, in a flat teeming with cooks, maids, servants and drivers. The scene was straight out of a Bollywood movie.

Yet, barely a few days after I was born, I was separated from my parents and sent away to live with my maternal grandparents, in an ordinary, rundown area in Mumbai, called Girgaon. My Nana and Nani were barely in their forties, had no other children (other than my mother) and they got custody of me.

Those who have heard this story have found it to be unusual and bizarre. Why did my young parents hand over their only child to my maternal grandparents, without any compelling factors? What could have been the unseen or unknown reasons for their unnatural behaviour? My parents were a happy couple, had two more children and doted over all of us. Why, then, did they choose to send me away? Who influenced them to do it? What were they made to believe and by whom?

For many years, I tried to figure out this riddle but got vague answers. My parents claimed they were too young and inexperienced to raise their first child and while they tried hard, my grandparents took over and that was that. Another time they said that they went on a world tour and when they returned, I refused to leave my grandparents and go back to them. When I asked my grandparents, they simply said, 'You became attached to us.' Honestly, I don't think anyone of them knew the real reasons. That's when I realised that some mysteries cannot be solved. This one, too, quietly slipped into the past and was forgotten.

It was forty years later that I had an epiphany. I understood that living with my grandparents was not some random act of insensitive parents; rather, a premeditated, secret, divine plan. It was my destiny to spend my childhood and formative years as an adult in the company of highly evolved spiritual souls who would significantly mould and influence me. My parents lived a worldly life. They were passionate about travelling, eating out at five-star hotels, going to the movies and socialising with friends. My grandparents lived a spiritual life. They kept to themselves, ate simple meals and visited temples and holy cities when they travelled.

It became clear to me that I had a unique destiny, and my grandparents would be my partners in helping me fulfil it. More about that, later.

My grandparents dedicated their lives to raising me. Growing up with them, I began to have unusual and profound spiritual experiences. As a young boy, I had dreams that took me decades to understand. In the temples and monasteries I visited, I had transformative experiences that completely altered my life. I met unusual and blessed men who made me realise the power of prophecies and karmic connections. It did not take me long to figure out that my life was a unique storybook, which was living out a destiny of its own. I was a mere witness.

As a young boy, I excelled in studies and began working in the family businesses from the age of sixteen. Luck, destiny and an innate sense of entrepreneurship brought me very early success. Even before I had turned thirty, I had overtaken my father in his business and established myself as a pioneering hosiery exporter from India. I then fortuitously started a dotcom venture that thrived beyond my expectations, and brought me fame, glory and money. Even though I had been a complete teetotaller while growing up, my new-found status resulted in my smoking and drinking occasionally. Also along with success came uninvited stress and anxiety.

Amidst all the mayhem, in the most unexpected way, the cave appeared and changed everything. I experienced the grace and love of my God and Guru and realised that with them around, I would receive everything I needed. My bad habits left me, and my professional work flourished. I found a magical balance being a spiritualist and a capitalist! There was no conflict in my being a businessman and a meditator. The cave became my portal through which I entered the golden world of deep spiritual blossoming and profound personal upliftment.

In this book, I wish you to be my fellow traveller, as I narrate some of the stories and experiences from my personal life. In the chapters that follow, I will share principles I have learned that I believe could benefit you as well. I have been the recipient of so much that I feel it is only fair that I share it with as many people as possible. I hope this book helps you on your journey of self-discovery.

All I request is that you have an open mind and an accepting heart!

TWO DREAMS

My Nana (born and raised in Mathura, Uttar Pradesh) and my Nani (born and raised in Beawar, Rajasthan) were the best parents I could have asked for. Selfless and straightforward, they invested considerable time in raising me and making sure that I was happy and fulfilled. My Nana was a successful businessman and we soon moved into a flat just a mile away from my parents' home. When I think about it, living with my Nana and Nani was the first of the many spiritual experiences that would grace my life.

At the age of ten, my Nani taught me a beautiful prayer for Lord Hanuman. She simply said, 'Say this prayer to Hanumanji, and he will take care of you.'

The prayer went:

Hanuman Pehelwan,
Barah baras ke jawan,
Haath mein laddoo,
Mukh mein paan,
Aap hamari raksha karna,
Aap ki raksha
Sri Ramchandrandji karenge.

Hanuman the Brave,
As young as twelve,
A laddoo in your hand,
A paan in your mouth,
Please protect me,
Just as you are protected,
By Lord Sri Ramchandraji.

I recited this prayer every night, for a long time after that.

We were a very tightly-knit family, and until the time I became a teenager, my grandparents and I slept in the same room. On the wall we faced while sleeping hung three striking posters. The picture in the centre was a beautiful one of Krishna and Radha. The one on the left was of Lord Ram renouncing his kingdom. On the right was a mesmerising portrait of Lord Hanuman, kneeling on one knee, opening his heart to reveal Lord Ram inside.

Every night, I would look at these pictures, say my prayers and fall asleep.

One night, when I was twelve, I had a vivid dream of Lord Krishna. He was in his 'Viraat Swaroop'—the universal form. The Krishna I saw in my dream was very different from the gentle, smiling, noble God who I saw in the poster each night. In my dream, Krishna's manifestation was overwhelming, overpowering and extremely scary! He was taller than a gigantic skyscraper and kept growing. All around him and within him appeared the pitch-dark universe, resplendent with brilliant stars and multi-coloured galaxies and planets. Infinite numbers of men, gods, animals, chariots and weapons seemed to be floating towards him and entering and exiting his humongous body.

I don't remember how long this dream lasted, but it remains as vivid and detailed in my mind today as from that night almost forty years ago.

After that dream, I always wondered—why was Krishna appearing in front of me and showing me his omnipotent self? Was He telling me that He was my God? Years later, I would find the answer to my question.

When I was thirteen years old, I had another dream. In it, I was walking up a gently sloping mountain road on a path laid with large grey concrete slabs, covered with smooth flowing water. As I climbed higher and neared the top of the mountain, I entered a cave-like temple which housed a small, red-hued Devi idol. I prayed to the Devi with my head bent. Then, my dream ended.

For many years, neither did I mention my dreams to anyone nor did I bother to figure out what they meant. The mountain cave did intrigue me since it seemed so real, but I had no one to discuss it with. So I let it be.

In the first year of my marriage, my wife Chhavi and I were casually chatting, and we talked about our childhood memories. I told Chhavi about these two dreams. While the Krishna dream astonished her, when she heard my dream about climbing the steep mountain, she immediately burst out saying, 'Alok, that is Vaishno Devi! You saw the idol of Mata Rani (the Goddess of Vaishno Devi).' Chhavi had lived in Delhi before moving to Mumbai after our marriage, and had been to the Vaishno Devi temple. She told me how she had entered a very narrow passage to get to the cave of Vaishno Devi with flowing water around her.

At the time when Chhavi told me about Vaishno Devi, I was twenty-two years old. It was almost ten years since I had had my dream. Both of us then decided to go on the pilgrimage soon.

There is a saying about Vaishno Devi that 'You can go to the temple only when you get a 'bulava' (invitation) from Mata Rani.'

True to the tale, it took me twenty-five years (literally) to go to Vaishno Devi and obtain a darshan of the Goddess. For many unknown reasons, we just never visited the temple until then.

At Vaishno Devi, when I finally walked on the giant grey slabs and covered the last few hundred feet up to the shrine enclosure for a darshan of Mata Rani, cool flowing water enveloped my feet. As I saw the small figurine of the Devi, I knew my dream had finally materialised. It was as if I was living my dream fully awake and with complete awareness.

Connecting the Dots

If you separate a child from his parents, he will be sorrowful. While that is what happened to me, I grew up amidst unbounded laughter and happiness. As an adult, when I reflected on this, it struck me that the most vulnerable moments in my life have served a larger purpose. I have gained more than I have lost. It all turned out to be not just better, but the best!

I realised that the 'sangat' or the company of people is very crucial when growing up. I was moulded by my grandparents, who were the most selfless people in the world. They deeply impacted and influenced me. I can assure you that the people you surround yourself with will influence the person you become. Keeping that in mind, whenever possible, seek the company of those who have a higher purpose in their lives and make others happy.

Exercise

Close your eyes and reflect on those moments when you thought all was lost and how you came through shining. How transient those moments seem now! If you could overcome such dark fears, you can overcome anything. Also, reflect on the company you keep. Do you think you need to reconsider some of the people you spend your precious time with? Stay with this thought for a few minutes.

BABA OF PURI

All through my school and college years, we had a never-ending line-up of visitors and guests at home. My Nana and Nani had plenty of outstation relatives who loved travelling and meeting one another. These guests bothered me with their noise and hyperactivity. I was an outstanding student, and my modus operandi was to study with rock and roll music blasting in the house. That obviously couldn't happen with guests around.

Many of our house guests simply lounged around the house and did nothing. It got worse when more relatives gathered from all over the city to meet the outstation visitors! Many of them were not well educated and constantly probed into my affairs. They got on my nerves.

We had our share of exciting guests too. There was a gentleman who showed up dead drunk one afternoon and made a fool of himself. Drinking, smoking and eating non-vegetarian food were all taboo for my grandparents (who called themselves Brijwasi or residents of the land of Krishna). They avoided people who were 'sharaabi, kabaabi aur juari' (drunks, meat-eaters and gamblers).

Whenever I was in the mood to play pranks, I would bring up the incident of the drunken uncle in the presence of my grandparents. They would go red in the face and ask me to change the topic quickly!

Like the drunken uncle, there was another male relative who was quite a comic character. He would come over to our house wearing shirts that were much too small for him (I called them women's blouses) and recite poetry about ovens (the kitchen appliance) or sometimes sing multiplication tables. I never figured out why he was the way he was. But I was a real 'badmaash' (naughty) teen and would start hooting when he was in his poetic or singing moods, much to the dismay of my Nani who would implore me to stay quiet!

The guests who got on my nerves the most were the holy men. My grandparents were very religious and would welcome all kinds of babas, gurus, soothsayers and fortune-tellers to our house. I could just about tolerate those who stayed for the day, but when these people stayed overnight, life became very miserable for me. I had to pretend to be respectful towards these people, even though in my heart of hearts, I wasn't.

When I was in the twelfth grade, sometime in the month of August, a troop of saffron-clad men from Puri (in Odisha) descended on our home. My grandparents welcomed them wholeheartedly and invited them to stay, much to my utter dismay.

I soon realised that the senior member of the troop was a dark, pot-bellied sage who wore nothing but a saffron-coloured dhoti. Everyone called him Baba. He sported a large number of beaded garlands and rings. I still remember something very odd about him. Even though he would continuously sweat, whenever I was near him, I would smell a pleasant perfume emanating from his body. I never figured out what that musk smell was. Each time I would pass by him, he would grin at me and ask, 'Baba, how are you?'

For reasons unknown to me, I quickly developed a deep dislike for Baba. His troop had laid siege to the hall that was pretty much my space. Their clothes were scattered all over and Baba had even created a small shrine in the room. Every time I entered my living room, it was bustling with people and confusion, and I hated the whole situation.

August in Mumbai is particularly hot and humid. One such torrid Sunday afternoon, as I exited my room and stepped into the hall, Baba looked into my eyes and said, 'Baba, it's so, so hot … Come here, Alok Baba, sit with me …'

I have no idea why I obeyed him and sat next to him. What transpired next shocked me and still sends shivers down my spine every time I think about it. Baba looked at me and said, 'Alok Baba, it's so hot, see my shaligram in my shrine—he is sweating too…!'

A shaligram is a small fossilised figurine stone which represents Lord Vishnu. The minute Baba said this, I turned towards the deity and saw that the little black rock was actually perspiring! For a minute, I thought this was an illusion or trick, but Baba gently took the shaligram out, wiped it with a handkerchief and put it back in the temple. A few seconds later, there were fresh beads of sweat around the shaligram.

I looked at Baba, smiled, got up, and left. There was nothing more to it.

The next day, my Nani told me that Baba was going back to Puri that afternoon and when I came back home from college, the house would be empty. Strangely, I wasn't excited at the thought of getting back my carefree life again. Just as I stepped out of my house to go to college, my eyes locked into Baba's eyes and I did a small pranam. His eyes twinkled, and he gently smiled and wished me goodbye.

After Baba had gone back, I would often enquire about him and ask my Nana to find out where he was. My Nana's sister, who lived in Kolkata, was the one who had introduced us to Baba and we often spoke to her to check on him.

I am not sure why my fondness for Baba kept growing every passing day, to the extent that I began missing him. Internally, while I very much wanted to see him again, externally, I maintained a stoic composure and pretended to be casually enquiring about him. My grandparents were surprised by my interest in Baba. I had never bothered finding out about the other holy men who had visited us in the past.

One Friday, I distinctly remember coming back home from college and going directly to meet my Nani, instead of disappearing into my room. I told my Nani in plain simple and direct words, 'Nani, I have to meet Baba. I want to meet him without any delay. Please figure it out and let's go as soon as possible.'

My Nani was surprised and pleased at the same time. She instantly called my Nana, and they began frantically calling up my Nana's sister in Kolkata to help them finalise the programme.

This incident is an example of how selflessly devoted my grandparents were to my whims and fancies. I just had to ask for something, and they moved heaven and earth to make it happen. My Nana was a relatively successful businessman who had an ongoing business, but when I wanted something, he dropped it all for me. In school, when I participated in Hindi elocution competitions, my Nana would spend days researching content that could be used for my speech, and even meet my Hindi teacher for consultation. My Nani would always motivate (and sometimes threaten) me to do my best. She made me realise my full capabilities.

Within five days of my asking to meet Baba, we were in a train bound for the holy city of Puri. My grandparents liked to travel by trains and enjoyed the sense of adventure that came with it. All through the long train ride, I yearned to meet Baba.

After a long, arduous journey of three days that seemed to last forever, we arrived at Puri railway station in the late afternoon. Without delay, we rushed to Baba's house located near the Jagannath Puri Temple. Baba was a leading dignitary of the temple. I remember the narrow lane that led to his home. My heart was pounding as I opened the gate and stepped inside.

'Baba?' I asked the first person I met, 'Where is Baba?'

The people assembled in the courtyard told me, 'Baba is in the temple. He is not here.'

Not wanting to waste another minute, I rushed towards the Jagannath Puri temple, with my grandparents trying to catch up. I had no clue where I would find Baba in the massive temple complex, but I just rushed anyway.

A pale golden hue had enveloped the city by the time we reached the temple premises. The skies were pink and blue. On evenings like these, my Nani would always say it was someone's marriage ceremony in heaven.

We proceeded to the main shrine inside. As we began climbing the stone stairs, I was stunned to see Baba standing right there, looking directly in my direction, as if he had been waiting on the steps for me. His eyes locked into mine and became moist. As I touched his feet in reverence, he pulled me up, hugged me and said, 'Alok Baba, what took you so long to come? Arre Baba, I have been waiting for months for you to come...'

The pure love and the innocent attraction I felt for Baba was inexplicable. We embraced each other for a long time. Later, we went back to his house and spent time with him for a couple of days. One day, he took me inside his room and began flipping slim ancient text scrolls to decipher my future. (There are many sacred and secret sciences in India that can shock and awe the most advanced non-believers and scientists.) He suddenly looked up and said, 'Arre Baba, you will become very famous!' Then he went silent and had tears in his eyes. I could not make out anything of what he was trying to communicate. All I knew was that we loved each other deeply.

Outside in the open courtyard, Baba would sit and hold court. When visitors would leave him money, he would fold the notes with the coin inside and fling it across the floor with his fingers, as if he was playing carrom. Money and wealth meant nothing to him.

An intriguing part of our trip was that Baba almost wholly ignored my grandparents all the while when we were with him. He barely even acknowledged their presence.

On the last day, just before departing, Baba hugged me and gently began to weep. I told him, 'Baba, why are you sad? We will keep meeting now!' Baba just looked at me and smiled. It seemed like he knew something that I did not.

One day, a few months after returning to Mumbai, I was stunned when my Nani told me that Baba was no more. He had left his body and taken samadhi. I then realised that Baba had wished me his last farewell when we had met before heading back to Mumbai. Maybe that is why he had made me visit him in Puri.

As I grieved, I also read the accolades and adulations for Baba that were pouring in. I was amazed to learn that Baba (Pandit Sadashiva Rath Sharma) was a world-renowned scholar of ancient Odia texts and had been conferred the Padma Shri Award in 1969 for his services to Odisha art.

So, who was Baba? Why had he suddenly come into my life, only to quickly disappear? What was our connection? Would I ever find out? Did it even matter? Honestly, it did not. For me, before and after, he was my loving, amazing and immortal Baba.

Connecting the Dots

Many of the people we meet in life may seem to appear randomly or by chance, but there is some connection, some link that makes such meetings happen. Often, we realise the importance of some people long after they have moved out of our lives. Even the people who trouble us or make us uncomfortable come into contact with us to give us a message and to correct us. We just have to be open to everyone and not make quick judgements.

In my case, Baba probably met me to teach me that it was foolish for me to judge people by their appearances and demeanour. Every person is special and can contribute to your personal upliftment. Baba came from nowhere and converted my dislike for him into inexplicable pure love. This served as an immortal lesson for me.

Exercise

Think of a couple of people whom you did not get along with and distanced yourself from. Could they have come into your life for some significant reason? If you had tolerated them, would you have gained something? Close your eyes for a few minutes and contemplate on this question. Can you be more open to people who come into your life from now on?

BANKEY BIHARI'S MAGIC

Vrindavan, a sleepy little hamlet in the state of Uttar Pradesh, is a wondrous place. Men in the city selling fruits and vegetables wear attractive eye make-up (surma) and speak very sweetly. The town has a sizable population of monkeys who often steal the belongings of innocent tourists and tease them. Cows, dogs, sages and widows throng the streets and have the first right of passage.

When a minor road accident takes place, the warring parties in all their angry overtones yell 'Radhe Radhe', instead of the usual angry words. 'Radhe Radhe' evokes Lord Krishna's sweet consort, Radha. Lord Krishna lived in Vrindavan, and his presence permeates everything in the town, even today.

My connection with Vrindavan is unique. My Nana was born and brought up in Mathura—an ancient Indian city located just a few miles away from Vrindavan. His family lived in a quaint temple house situated right on the banks of the Yamuna river at a place called Swami Ghat. Since I grew up with my Nana and Nani, I visited Mathura often, usually during my vacations. I distinctly remember taking boat rides across the Yamuna and being in awe of the godmen who roamed the innumerable ghats of the holy city.

It was in nearby Vrindavan that I discovered the most amazing and mystical temple I have ever visited—that of Lord Bankey Bihari. Tucked away in the labyrinths of the narrow Vrindavan gullies, Bankey Bihari's temple is where I felt instantly uplifted. Bankey Bihari is the dark idol deity of Lord Krishna in child form. He is always adorned with beautiful flowers, jewellery, the finest of garments, and it appears as if his shining diamond eyes follow you as you move around in the shrine.

The temple and its folklore are unique. Since the presiding deity is Lord Krishna depicted as a child, the founder of the temple—Swami Haridas—decided not to have the usual early morning aarti (prayers) which is standard in all Hindu temples. Swami Haridas wanted the child Krishna to sleep, undisturbed.

When you obtain a darshan of Bankey Bihari, you instantly feel a lift of energy, and even more when you focus on his eyes. Which is why, as per folklore, the temple curtain continually opens and closes, so that mortals don't get mesmerised by Bankey Bihari's eyes! Another tale is about Bankey Bihari being so innocent that when he makes eye contact with his devotees who show him their love, he walks out of his temple and follows them!

I grew up visiting temples since it was something my Nani enjoyed doing. Our house on Peddar Road is a few minutes away from the famous Mahalaxmi and Babulnath temples in Mumbai and we visited them often. My Nani lured me with 'garam garam pakoras' that were sold outside Mahalaxmi so that I would accompany her. Later, I began to love the serenity and peace of these temples.

While I cherish most of the temples I have visited, I have never felt such a strong attraction to any other temple as I have experienced for Bankey Bihari. What made me fall in love with Bankey Bihari at first sight? He had not done anything for me, and yet I felt so connected and grateful towards him. He didn't even look like the Krishna I had dreamt of when I was twelve.

In any case, this temple became 'my temple'. As I graduated, got married and started working in my father's socks factory, I visited Bankey Bihari every year. Something told me that he would always be there for me when I needed him the most.

As destiny would have it, my faith would soon be tested.

After my graduation from Sydenham College, Mumbai, I joined my father's socks factory in Lower Parel. While I was in college, I realised that I had a strong inclination towards entrepreneurship, and my Nana helped me indulge in it, fully! I successfully ran a number of small business ventures and also worked with my Nana in his business.

It was in my father's factory that I came face-to-face with the complex, challenging and daunting opportunities of large-scale business operations. From my early childhood, I have experienced a divine grace that has guided me to reach higher and higher levels in the work I have attempted. It was the same grace that blessed me when I began work in the socks factory. Just a few years after joining, I had pioneered the concept of socks exports from India and was almost at par with the turnover of the division my father oversaw— something that he had spent twenty long years achieving. Even before I turned thirty, I had become quite successful, and had amply proved my entrepreneurial qualities.

Or so I thought.

Amidst all this success, there was something in my life which wasn't working well at all. My uncles (father's brothers) who had been working in the factory for decades, began to despise my rapid success. Even though they were equal partners in the business and enjoyed unprecedented financial dividends thanks to my efforts, every passing day, they systematically began to make my life miserable and painful. I was not given a salary and denied recognition as someone officially working in the business.

One day, my will power to continue working, amidst all the problems, simply broke down. A particularly mean incident completely shattered me. That day, late in the afternoon, as I walked between the factory buildings, I remembered my Bankey Bihari. With a heavy but sincere heart, I prayed for five things at once: 'Bihariji, please get me out of here. Give me a business of my own that requires no money; something that makes me use my brains; my work should get me to meet the best people in the world; I need all of this now.'

It will amaze you to know that Bankey Bihari did not just listen to my prayer, but also granted me all the five wishes I had asked him that day.

A few months later, one early morning, I received a call from the factory telephone operator, Mr Salvi, on the intercom. Salvi had been working with my father for twenty years and had a distinctive style of communication. He said, 'Alok Babu, there is a man called Gopala Krishna here to meet you. He says he wants to sell computers to us. He is very dark.' (This was Salvi's style. He often described a visitor's physical appearance on the phone, mostly in unflattering terms, sometimes within earshot of the visitor.)

I have come to realise that sometimes luck and providence come directly to your doorstep and yet the untrained mind chooses to close the door on them. I told Salvi, 'Tell this guy to meet the IT team. I don't need to buy computers.' Salvi called back and said, 'Gopala says he only wants to meet you.' I was irritated, but reluctantly agreed and asked Salvi to send Gopala down to my cabin on the production floor.

The moment I met Gopala Krishna (GK), I knew he was different. His eyes twinkled when he spoke, and he had a very infectious enthusiasm. He said, 'Mr Kejriwal, I want to suggest that you make a website for your socks business. You can find global buyers for your amazing products that remain undiscovered by the world. Your website will help you connect those buyers with your company.'

I guess I was so daft that I still didn't get it. I did not connect the dots when Gopala spoke about the internet. It was only a few days later that I realised—the internet was the secret key I was searching for to create a brand new business for myself and Gopala Krishna was trying to hand me precisely that.

The next two years were nothing short of magic. I quit my father's business and started a contests website called contests2win.com. That idea became wildly successful. I raised venture capital from some of the best known financiers in the world. The company later launched a joint venture with Softbank in China. In the years to come, the Chinese business I had started would be acquired by Walt Disney and the Indian business acquired by two venture capital firms.

In my first book, *Why I Stopped Wearing My Socks*, I describe the incredible and miraculous journey of my life just after I made this prayer. The book traces how I created an extremely valuable business from just an idea and how I built a new age digital enterprise without any relevant training or background whatsoever. Even today, I cannot understand how everything fell into place so perfectly, and what made me—an MCom graduate—become a successful internet pioneer. When the puzzle becomes overbearing to solve, I give up thinking. And just then, the answer pops up—'Bankey Bihari's grace and love!'

In less than eight years of starting from scratch, I had succeeded beyond my wildest imagination and had become quite famous, too. (Baba of Puri had predicted this to me way back when I had met him.)

Fifteen odd years later, I managed to understand what happened: I had prayed to Bankey Bihari—the dark-complexioned Krishna—to help me redeem my life. It was he who had sent to me the dark-complexioned Gopala Krishna (with sparkling eyes!). And to make sure you understand the extent of Bankey Bihari's grace—he made all my five wishes come true! He helped me exit the socks business; started up my dotcom business with literally no money; leveraged my brains to build a business; made me meet the who's who of the world, and all this instantly, soon after I made my wish.

Connecting the Dots

Prayer is supremely powerful. It doesn't matter if you believe in a God or a spirit or if you are an atheist. The possibility of finding redemption in prayer always exists. Just emptying yourself and acknowledging your deepest vulnerabilities will give you the power and energy to help yourself.

For the spiritually inclined, we all know how powerful thoughts and wishes can be. If you are sincere, truthful and dedicated, your prayers can achieve a great deal for you.

Exercise

Close your eyes and spend three minutes praying to whomever you believe in. It could just be a higher power or energy. Pray from your heart and be grateful for what you have received. Afterwards, check your state of mind and evaluate how you felt before and after your prayer. If possible, make this a daily habit!

THE MAGIC OF KRIYA

'Alok-ji, we have only four months of cash left,' gasped Gopala Krishna (GK), my Chief Strategy and Technology Officer (CTO) and tech partner at my first startup—contests2win.com. I still cannot forget that spine-chilling day in the office, in the year 2001, a year-and-a-half after we had launched. GK had joined me as CTO, and we had gotten off to a brilliant start as one of the first dotcom businesses of India that had made a deep impact in a nascent and underdeveloped market.

In a short period, I had managed to work with all the top brands in the country. My company had received funding by none other than ICICI, Softbank and Newscorp and had begun generating healthy revenues. It employed some of the most innovative minds in India and was a global pioneer in the concept of adver-gaming (gaming with brands). Just when it seemed 'too good to be true', disaster struck.

The dotcom bust descended upon us in early 2001 like a lightning thunderbolt in a freak storm. By the middle of that year, most 'dotcoms' had become 'dot-gones'. No one wanted to work with or be associated with internet businesses, which overnight seemed to be silly whimsical fads. While our employees loved our company, many of them came up to me and said, 'Alok Sir, can we change the name of our business from dotcom to something else? Our parents and relatives are pressuring us to leave such companies.' Our venture capitalists (VCs) were near bankrupt and began to wind down. To top it all, 80 per cent of our clients for whom we did business were dotcom brands themselves, and almost all of them vanished overnight.

My younger daughter was born on the same day that I got my first venture capital funding. And then, a few months later, my business came under a lot of pressure. Life at home became super-challenging. I had to support our very young family while my wife Chhavi was busy raising our two girls. My father, for whom I had worked for several years, was no longer responsible for me. I had abandoned his business, and there was no going back. As far as education was concerned, I had a Master of Commerce (MCom) degree from Mumbai University that wasn't worth much. It was like being in a choppy ocean without a lifejacket or a boat. It was up to me to figure out how to survive.

When one enters the dark tunnel of negativity, there seems to be no exit from it. Things just begin to get darker and bleaker. Add stress to it, and you have the recipe for a deadly killer. As my business began to crash and burn, I started to think of all the worst outcomes possible if I had to shut my business down. My mind played cunning tricks on me. More than the sadness of failing and losing the opportunity to get a brand new business idea going, I was more upset about how society, my family members and community would perceive me and make fun of me. Just imagining their ugly taunts gave me the shivers. If there was a hell on earth, I had found it.

One late afternoon, Sunita Shah—a college friend of mine with whom I had been in irregular touch—called and asked me how I was doing. I rattled off my story, in the hope of feeling better.

Sunita said, 'Alok, I have no clue what dotcom means or what you do! I can't figure out how to help your business. But I can offer an idea that may just change everything for the better.'

When you are in dire straits, you don't negotiate, argue or contemplate. You just surrender. 'Tell me what I should be doing, Sunita,' I pleaded.

Sunita asked me to attend the Art of Living's Basic Course that was being organised at the Woodlands Building on Peddar Road. It was a few buildings away from my home and she strongly recommended it. I immediately agreed and signed up.

When good things are supposed to happen, everything falls into place. As a hardened entrepreneur who had met hundreds of people, I was choosy about the people I liked and respected. I made quick judgements about people and rarely changed them. (This has been a major personal flaw that has slowly ironed itself out over the years.) The teacher for that Art of Living course was Sanjiv Sarin—a senior general manager with Cadbury India. Sunita, my friend, had played her cards well. She knew I would in all likelihood be impressed by Sanjiv and his corporate background, and would probably complete the course.

Some distinct memories, however trivial, last forever. I clearly remember entering Sanjiv's home and hearing one of the sweetest sitar compositions I had ever heard. It was Craig Pruess playing 'Welcome Home'. My heart melted even before I sat down.

I attended the programme diligently and committed myself to it. On the second day, Sanjiv said, 'We are now going to experience the Sudarshan Kriya. It's an amazing experience, so enjoy it and don't try and control your thoughts and emotions. Just let them flow...'

Sudarshan Kriya is a gift that Sri Sri Ravishankar received after a period of prolonged silence and intense meditation on the banks of the Tunga river in Shimoga, Karnataka. It is a yogic breathing technique, infused with a unique divine energy that is directly experienced by the practitioner.

My first experience of the Sudarshan Kriya remains one of the most precious and unforgettable experiences of my life. To this day, I vividly remember all my feelings about that fantastic session. To preserve the sanctity of this ancient and priceless technique, I will not describe my experiences in detail. All I will say is that even if you are a non-believer, you must experience the Sudarshan Kriya once in your life!

Just after the Kriya ended, as we were leaving, Sanjiv said something strange. He mentioned that the Kriya had a detoxifying effect on our body and its nervous system, and that we had to hydrate ourselves to let the toxins flow out. He repeated these instructions, implying how important they were.

The drive from the Woodlands building to my house on Peddar Road takes less than three minutes. A minute or two after I had got into my car and made the U-turn at Kemps Corner, I began to feel violently sick. I managed to drive the car a few metres, parked it on the left side kerb and began to throw up, repeatedly. It felt like the buried poisons embedded in me were being removed from my body. Over and over again, I experienced an overwhelming feeling to expel everything from inside my system. I couldn't understand what was happening to me. Just an hour ago, I had been fine and now it seemed like I was extremely unwell. A few minutes later, after I had settled down, I drove home and drank plenty of water as Sanjiv had instructed. If I had toxins accumulated inside me, I was going to get rid of them with a vengeance!

The next day at work, I knew something had changed. There was a shift in my energy levels. I felt purer and lighter. I felt as if a glow of positivity had enveloped me. It could have been psychological or just a placebo effect, I do not know. What I did know was that I felt different.

In the gruelling weeks that followed, GK and I struggled to find a solution to our cash flow problem. GK had a fantastic insight and gave me a new business direction to pursue—he asked me to focus on clients and get advances from them as opposed to chasing VCs who had vanished from the scene. For some odd reason, those words completely transformed me. Maybe my experience with Sudarshan Kriya had made me more receptive and open-minded. Probably, I had accepted my vulnerability and wanted to overcome it. Whatever the change was, when GK gave me directions, I took up the challenge immediately, and things began to improve. I became a hard-driving salesman. In a few months, things had changed. A year later, there was no turning back. We successfully survived the dotcom bust.

Circa 2020. It's been nineteen years since my first Sudarshan Kriya. It has become part of my daily ritual, and I have rarely missed practising it over all these years! What motivated me to never stop doing my Kriya? The overwhelming benefits of focus, calmness, super intuition, creativity and a feeling of contentment and happiness. As far as business goes, contests2win.com continues to thrive and has spun out many other successful companies since.

When I look back and relive those horrific days and months of the dotcom bust, I wonder about the strange coincidence of everything changing for me just after I did my first Sudarshan Kriya. I guess I had all the ingredients I needed to pull through the bust; the Sudarshan Kriya just made me see them.

Connecting the Dots

Any practice that helps delink the mind from worries and stress is a must-do. It could be exercising, a hobby, being with nature, serving people and, of course, meditation. The key is to be regular and committed to it.

I've realised that the mind gravitates towards the negative more often than the positive. There are many reasons why this happens. In any case, to prevent your mind from becoming its enemy, it is essential to engage yourself in activities that are refreshing and positive. Meditation is the most effective method I have encountered.

When we are in a positive, happy state of mind, we become open to ideas, experiments and new directions. That's all we need to succeed!

Exercise

Think of those things that make you instantly happy. It could be your family, your work, your hobby, memories or an experience that you cherish. Close your eyes and spend five minutes thinking about them. Then gently open your mind and observe your mind. Do you feel more positive? If the answer is no, then the things you thought that brought you happiness are false. I would urge you to try once more.

If your answer is yes, you have found a secret solution to help yourself whenever you need to. Also, try and experience any sort of meditation once, if you can.

SHUTTERS ON THE BEACH

After narrowly escaping the nerve-wracking dotcom bust, things began to get better for me quickly. In the next five years, I was able to launch two new companies—mobile2win India and mobile2win China—that focused on mobile promotions and leveraging brands and media. In India, there were very few internet entrepreneurs remaining, and I was one of the fortunate ones whose ventures were global and profitable. This experience generated tremendous amounts of positive PR and goodwill for me. I earned the recognition of being a successful Indian internet entrepreneur.

In 2003, on a whim, I decided to travel to Los Angeles (LA) and invited my colleague Dinesh Gopalakrishna aka Dinu to accompany me. Dinu has been with me since I launched contests2win and we are like brothers in arms. My plan was for us to attend E3—the massive global gaming exposition that takes place in LA every year. E3 is the Mecca for game developers, and I decided to check it out and figure if there was something in gaming that I could build a new business around.

If there are prizes for planning the worst trips in the world, I would have won first place for my LA trip. When I look back and think about it, it makes me shudder! I had never visited LA before but assumed it was an accessible city to get around. I refused to pay attention to planning our travel details. There was no researching of hotels nor any attention paid to logistics (the internet had still not kicked in fully, so international travel plans had to be through emails and faxes). Little did I know that I was in for the nightmare of my life!

After we landed, Dinesh and I checked into a three-star hotel near Los Angeles International Airport (LAX) that turned out to be miles away from the convention halls. LAX is where you fly in or fly out from—not where you stay! Apart from being far away from the city, it was also sleazy and dangerous. Each night, Dinu and I would witness scenes outside our hotel that would make us shiver. To add to the mayhem, since private taxis were atrociously expensive (there was no Uber back then), we had to travel by public transport. On the LA buses, we were continuously spooked by random strangers who were usually drunks or drug addicts. It was a hell-of-a-trip, pun intended. To top it all, the E3 exhibition turned out to be a damp squib and irrelevant for my company's business.

I was very disappointed with LA and I desperately wanted something exciting to happen. One afternoon, I told Dinesh, 'Dinu, let's hit the LA beaches and explore them. Let's find all the places where they filmed the superhit serial *Baywatch*.' (*Baywatch* was an extremely popular TV serial back then.)

To get to the beach, we boarded multiple buses that seemed to take forever before we arrived at Santa Monica Pier. Once we were there, we immediately hit the sands. Much to our regret, it wasn't like *Baywatch* at all. Amateur swimmers were swimming rather expertly and did not need rescuing. I was sorely disappointed.

On the positive side, Santa Monica was calm and beautiful. We were mesmerised by the deep, peaceful, light blue Pacific Ocean that hugged the city.

As we walked the expanse of the beach in a melancholic mood, I came across a stunning resort located on the beach. Most of the hotels were on Ocean Avenue that ran between the beach and the city, but this fantastic resort was located right on the beach.

I stared at the property and could see people standing on the balconies of some of the rooms, staring out at the ocean. It seemed as if they owned the beach. How lucky they were! Just as I walked past it, I silently muttered to myself, 'Wow … what an amazing place to stay! I wonder who gets to stay in places like these. How do you get so lucky?'

As the evening descended on us, Dinu and I leisurely walked down some of the main streets of Santa Monica and ate dinner at a restaurant tucked away in a building garage. I distinctly remember that the moment I stepped into Santa Monica, I was smitten by it. It seemed just the place where I wanted to spend more time in. Something shifted in my heart when I was there. LA didn't seem to be such a hopeless place after all.

A couple of days later, while flying out from LA, as the plane took off, I looked out of the window, saw the ocean surf and remembered Santa Monica. I had a pang of regret that I hadn't spent much time there and wasn't going to be returning soon. My heart was heavy and a bit sad.

How little I knew what Santa Monica had in store for me!

Two years later, in 2005, IBM India invited me to participate in a closed room discussion on the future of business with the internet. Shanker Annaswamy had just taken over as the country head of IBM in India and was presiding over this conference.

In public discussions, I speak from the heart and share my unfiltered views. I have never understood what the term 'politically correct' really means. (In my opinion, everything that's wrong in the world has its roots in politics. Then, how can something be 'correct' in it?) My habit of sharing my ideas and thoughts without sugar-coating them often makes me come across as very direct, and sometimes as a rude person.

At the IBM conference in Mumbai, I was my pure, unadulterated, no holds barred self. I predicted that stodgy companies like IBM (the host) would be extinct and the future belonged to companies whose consumers did the marketing, not salaried men in suits. I shared how the internet was all about democracy and giving away things, including software for free, unlike companies (like IBM) that relied on long-term annuity revenues built on antiquated business models. In most conferences, like this one, I was the guy that embarrassed everyone, especially the hosts.

A few weeks later, I was surprised when I received a call from IBM Bangalore. The person said that my feedback was amongst the best they had received and IBM in the US wanted me to participate in a smaller conference on the same subject. Would I be interested in going? I said 'Yes' without blinking an eyelid! In my mind, I gave myself a mental pat. Being brutally truthful had some benefits after all!

A week later, I got my travel itinerary, and when I read that I was flying to LA, I chuckled. It seemed that LA and I were not done with each other, just yet.

IBM was a super host, and I arrived in LA having slept all through the flights in business class. (That was my first business class trip and I hadn't paid for it. A classic entrepreneur high!) At the airport, a driver in a sharp black suit greeted me and walked me to his sleek black stretch limousine. I asked him, 'Where are we going? Do you know where the hotel is?'

'Santa Monica,' he replied, politely.

When I heard Santa Monica, I smiled, and my heart danced. How coincidental could this be? Could this lucky start be the indication of even better things to follow?

The drive took about half-an-hour, and I had dozed off when I heard someone calling me. We had arrived at the hotel. As I got out of the car and walked into the lobby, I was shocked. My heart started to beat faster. I instantly recognised where I was. The hotel I had just entered was on Santa Monica beach! This property was Shutters on the Beach, the same hotel I had come across a couple of years ago while walking with Dinesh and wondering, 'Who would stay in places like these?' Instantly, it became crystal-clear to me. This time, it was I who was staying here, not any one else. As I walked towards the reception to check-in, I had goosebumps that refused to settle down.

The charming receptionist greeted me and said, 'Welcome to Shutters on the Beach. Have you been here before?'

I looked at her, smiled, and gently nodded in agreement. In my mind, I answered, 'Yes, I have been here before, but as an admirer, not as a guest!' My heart yearned to tell her the real story.

My room was gorgeous. IBM had spared no cost to treat its guests well. Just as the sun began to set, I stepped out onto the private balcony attached to my room and stared at the surf, sand and ocean. Was this a dream, I wondered?

The next morning, I entered a small suite that only had eight participants. We were the few selected 'thinkers' that IBM had invited from all over the world. I was stunned by the privilege and prestige bestowed on me. As we greeted and introduced each other, a tall, authoritative lady walked in, followed by her small team. They were from IBM and were going to listen to our chatter, with little intervention. When the discussions started, I quickly realised that the lady was undoubtedly the sharpest person in the room. She was Gini Rometty, who later became the CEO of IBM! Every time I think about that session, I cannot believe that the future CEO of IBM would be sitting with me for hours, taking notes and asking me for clarifications on some of the points I had made.

For two days, we debated, argued and brainstormed on the future of the internet and the many possibilities that lay ahead. The cosy conference room had side doors that directly led to the beach outside. Often we took breaks on the patio outdoors. While standing there, strangers walking on the beach would greet me and look at the hotel in awe. Every time this happened, I would remember myself, doing the same, just a couple of years ago. It was an overwhelming feeling.

As the conference came to an end, I reflected deeply on how this trip of mine to LA was so different from the last one. This time I felt so fulfilled and successful. Santa Monica had treated me well. What was my connection with this city? Was my sweet love affair with Santa Monica over? This connection was a secret that would remain hidden from me for a few more years.

Connecting the Dots

What we wish for, often gets fulfilled. In Hindu tradition, the elders ask the young to be careful with their words and wishes. They often cite the meaning of Tathastu. Tathastu is a Sanskrit word combining the words tat (so) + astu (happen or be it) meaning 'may things happen as per your wish'. So what we wish for is to be expressed with utmost care.

I have experienced my words and thoughts coming true, even some of the negative ones. This principle is the reason I try to be very careful with my words and wishes.

Is this some sort of superstition or magic? I think it's quite the opposite. All of us originate from the universe, and when we wish for things, sometimes, nature reorganises itself to make a few of those wishes come true. On this subject, I like my guru Sri Sri Ravishankar's viewpoint. He says while we can have all our dreams fulfilled, the universe gives preference to wishes that work for the larger good of people as opposed to only personal, selfish desires. Thus, wishing to own a car rental business (hence employing many people) may be answered faster than a wish of just owning a car! (Note: I haven't tried that yet.)

Exercise

Close your eyes and think of those strange and sweet coincidences when your wishes have quickly come true. Did you make any special effort for it? Or was it just an innocent wish that magically got fulfilled? If you have the power to make things happen, can you wish well for others, too? Can you reject negative thoughts and instead wish for positive outcomes for yourself and others, knowing very well that they will eventually come true?

Make a strong, positive and inclusive wish and surrender it to the universe.

INDIAN SCHOOL OF BUSINESS, HYDERABAD

As a startup entrepreneur who had almost perished in the dotcom bust, I trained myself to be very frugal. That meant maximising every rupee spent and extending the 'paisa vasool' (stretching money) concept to everything I did. Take, for instance, travelling to different cities for work. I followed a self-imposed diktat called 'First In, Last Out', meaning that I would always take the first flight into a city and the last one back. How was this paisa vasool? Well, it was a simple hack to maximise time in the city I was travelling to, so that I could do more business.

The only time I broke my own rule was in 2006 when I had to travel to Hyderabad for a panel on entrepreneurship, being organised by the Indian School of Business (ISB). I cannot remember now why I didn't book the first flight and instead chose to go by the second one.

On reaching Mumbai airport, I discovered that my flight was delayed. As I did the maths in my head, I calculated that even if the plane did leave at the delayed time, I would probably not make it in time to the panel discussion. It made no sense for me to travel.

Embarrassed by my foolishness and miscalculation, I called my wife and said, 'Chhavi, my flight is very late. I made a mistake not taking the earlier one, so I'm thinking of going back to the office.'

What Chhavi said shocked me. She said, 'Alok, you stepped out of the house to go to work, so do your work and come back. There is no returning midway.' She disconnected the phone. I had never heard Chhavi speak to me like this before. It was almost like she was telling me to go to Hyderabad, even though it seemed illogical to do so.

So, I took the flight and reached the ISB campus a few minutes after my panel was supposed to have begun. As it often happens, the earlier programmes were running late, and that helped me make it to my session on time. The discussion was about entrepreneurship and I was given a hero's welcome since I had recently exited my previous company, mobile2win, through its sale to the Walt Disney Corporation.

On the panel, I noticed a distinguished young man in an expensive designer jacket. The more I looked at him, the more he resembled one of the male models from the Raymond's 'Complete Man' campaign or straight out of GQ magazine. He spoke slowly, with deeply measured words and with an air of authority. I quickly scanned his name placard and found out that he was Rahul Khanna from Clearstone Venture Partners. I had neither heard of Rahul nor of his firm. But what he said next got all my attention.

In a very sophisticated, convincing and authoritative tone, Rahul described the tremendous opportunity of online gaming and how India would mimic China where millions of consumers played very successful massive multiplayer online games (MMOG) in plush internet cafes. The gaming companies that had launched these businesses in China had become multi-billion dollar ventures and had listed themselves in the local stock exchanges. Rahul then quoted numbers, demographics, user preferences and other triggers that would fire up gaming in India, the same way as it had happened in China.

As I listened to him, my heart began to thump faster. Here was a VC talking about my domain! I was the guy who had pioneered gaming in India and what Rahul had so eloquently spoken about, was entirely about my space. Even as my ego took a solid beating, my mind raced. As a trained entrepreneur, I knew that if a VC was diving deep into a domain, he was most likely to finance it or announce a deal in it, very soon.

Just as all kinds of fears began to pass through my mind, I felt my phone vibrate. When I quietly peeked at it, I saw an SMS from Ganesh Rengaswamy who was sitting in the audience. Ramesh worked at Greylock Partners—a prominent global VC and was responsible for its Indian business. Ganesh and I knew each other well. Ganesh's message confirmed my deepest fears. It read, 'Alok, seems like Rahul is going to announce a gaming deal very soon. Better watch out my friend, your space is getting competition.'

I hung on to every word that Rahul said, bracing myself for the funding announcement of a local gaming company.

Oddly, no such announcement came. Rahul concluded his presentation commenting on how India could become one of the most significant opportunities for internet gaming in the world.

As soon as the panel session ended, I met Rahul and introduced myself. He had heard of me. When I found out more details about him, I was happy to learn that he was a South Mumbai lad like me. I had met his sister and her friends, with whom I had attended Nani Palkhiwala's famous budget speeches at the Cricket Club of India. As I left the ISB Campus, I promised to meet Rahul in Mumbai very soon.

The very next week, I was in the plush, elegant Clearstone office on the seventeenth floor at the Oberoi Towers, with a majestic view of the Arabian Sea. Like an emperor, Rahul sat at the single desk that occupied his office suite and quizzed me on the future of gaming and how I thought the Indian market would evolve. While I had a conservative approach, I shared Rahul's bullishness about the internet and its potential in India. I had begun preparing for my fourth startup—Games2win—that was all about consumer gaming and excitedly shared its plans with Rahul. My vision for Games2win was a global, casual gaming business built out of India.

After this first meeting, we met again, several times. Our meetings got more intense, and Rahul and I thrashed out details of a 'go-to-market' plan for Games2win. I had already begun discussions with Mahesh Khambadkone from Bangalore to join Games2win as CTO and Cyrus Oshidar from Mumbai to be the Creative Director of the company.

I introduced both of them to Rahul who spent quality time with them, understanding their backgrounds and skill sets. Rahul seemed convinced that Games2win had the team and execution plan to be a winning business. In less than three months, Clearstone wrote out a term sheet for the company, to invest about four million US dollars in a company that had not even started up! A month later, as soon as all the complicated documents were signed, eighteen crore rupees landed in my company's bank account.

I was ready to go.

In all my past experiences of raising capital, funding businesses, and even selling two companies, I had never seen a deal close this fast. The speed and the frictionless connect between me, Rahul and Clearstone was surreal. The transaction seemed propelled by factors that went beyond normal. It was as if an invisible force was behind it, determined to make it happen.

The day after the deal was inked, I asked Rahul, 'Rahul, when you made that speech at the ISB, I thought you were going to announce a deal that day. Were you?'

Rahul looked at me and with his classic grin, said, 'Alok, I was going to announce a deal! I had written out a term sheet to Kreeda Games (another Indian gaming company) the night before I flew out, and the promoter and I had agreed that I would announce the deal at the ISB summit. That morning, when I landed at Hyderabad and switched on my phone, I saw a message from the company promoter that he was not interested in my offer. The deal was off. So, I had a speech but no deal!' (Kreeda Games did raise money from IDG Capital a few months later but could not pivot its business and had to shut down its operations three years later.)

I was amazed to hear the sequence of events that Rahul mentioned. I had goosebumps when I remembered how that morning I had actually almost cancelled my trip to Hyderabad. It was only Chhavi's prompt that had made me travel. While I was lucky to have made the trip, what were the odds that on a panel at that same conference, there would be a venture capitalist, fully invested and committed to funding an Indian gaming company, with a deal that had just fallen through? Someone I would be able to convince to accept an alternate and better investment option, which he would buy into and fund within three months?

For me, it was crystal clear. The circumstances of my ISB trip were another classic case of divine intervention that had favoured me. While I did realise how fortunate I was to have my new company quickly funded and without much effort, I did not fathom the deeper connection of Clearstone Ventures becoming my partner. As it turned out, this was a part of a much larger plan that the universe had in store for me. Soon, I would find out everything.

Connecting the Dots

If you carefully examine coincidences, some of them will not seem to be coincidences at all. Many epic events in our lives are preordained, even though they appear to look like luck or chance. If you train yourself to pay more attention to such occurrences, you can take advantage of the subtle signals and signs that are always coming your way. The trick is not to resist suggestions or cues via events or by people.

Exercise

Close your eyes and think of those moments when you have been very lucky and fortunate. Is there a pattern you can discern amongst such events? Were there changes in your life that precipitated these luck-filled incidents? Were they random or based on something more profound that you may have missed? Did you take up the advice of someone on a whim and did it work well for you? What made you follow that person?

Even if no clear answer emerges, the next time you get lucky or have a happy coincidence, observe the situation a bit more deeply and with a sense of wonder. Maybe you will find a deep insight you have missed all these years! Many spiritualists suggest maintaining a daily diary of the routine events of life. If you record coincidences or unexplained incidents in it, reading your diary later can help you identify recurring patterns.

WELCOME TO THE PARTY!

Soon after Games2win received funding in March 2007, my investor and board member Rahul Khanna called me. He said, 'Alok, Clearstone has its headquarters in the US. You must go there, meet the partners and team of Clearstone and interact with them so that they can get to know you and your business better.'

That sounded like a logical thing to do, and I asked Rahul to help me plan my trip.

A couple of weeks later, Rahul emailed me introductions to his partners in the US, and we agreed on a meeting schedule. When I read the office address, my heart began to beat wildly. Clearstone Venture Partners had its offices in the centre of Santa Monica. I could not believe my luck that I was going to be back in my favourite city once again!

My meeting was at 4 p.m. on a Friday. I had never done a business meeting with a venture capital firm in the US before, so I dressed formally, wearing a black jacket, blue shirt and khaki trousers. The Clearstone office entrance on 4th Street, Santa Monica, was charming and quaint. I took the elevator to the fourth floor. Just as the lift doors opened and I stepped out, I met a huge, pot-bellied man in a white t-shirt and jeans. He seemed to have red wine spilt all over his shirt! He grinned at me and bellowed, 'Welcome to the party!'

I was bewildered. Party? I thought I was there to meet my investors and board members formally. I didn't remember being invited to a party.

As I walked into the lobby area, I was taken aback. The place was vast, and it was buzzing with dozens of people hanging around, drinks in their hands. There was music playing. It did seem to be a party!

I did my best to blend in and helped myself to a nice big glass of dark red wine. I told myself, 'When in California, do as the Californians do'—which meant enjoying wine!

As I patiently waded through the room, I did not recognise anyone. Later, I came to know that the party was a regular 'Friday Mixer' that Clearstone organised for its portfolio companies and its partners and guests, to help them network and unwind as the weekend began.

Just as I was finishing my second glass of wine, a tall, distinguished, spectacled man spotted me, came up and asked, 'Hey, nice to meet you! I haven't seen you around, so I'm guessing you've come for the first time?'

I was relieved to have met someone and quickly rattled off, saying, 'Yeah! I'm Alok from Games2win India, and I've come here to meet the Clearstone Partners. My company just got funded and Rahul Khanna, the India partner of Clearstone, asked me to come here.'

The man chuckled and said, 'Oh my! You've come from India for our mixer! That's amazing. I'm sure you will enjoy our party.'

Neither of us spoke about my business or what the purpose of my visit was.

A few minutes later, the same man met me again and asked, 'Alok, what do you do? What is your passion?'

The wine had begun playing tricks on my mind, and my jetlag wasn't helping either. I was tired and mumbled rather impatiently, 'Sir, I just told you! I'm the guy Clearstone funded in India to make online games!'

The man smiled and quickly said, 'Oh, forget about business and work! Tell me, what are your real interests? What is your hobby? What do you do when you are not working?'

For some strange reason, I instinctively blurted out, 'I have spiritual interests. I like to meditate.'

The man's face lit up, and he said, 'Wow! That's nice! Do you have a guru? Who taught you meditation?'

I replied, 'Well, I've learned meditation from an organisation called the Art of Living, whose founder is Sri Sri Ravishankar, my guru. He is a contemporary spiritual leader from India...'

Just as I said these words, the man interrupted me, flashed a broad grin and asked me to follow him to his office.

In my entrepreneurial career, I've seen all sorts of offices, but when I entered this man's office, I was taken aback. The office was enormous and classy and I realised that this person wasn't someone ordinary at Clearstone.

After we entered the room, the man said, 'I am Bill Elkus. I am the founder of Clearstone Venture Partners. Now, let me show you something you will find interesting.' Bill walked me to his ornate mahogany desk and opened the second drawer. Then he took out some pictures and showed them to me excitedly. Bill said, 'Alok, look at these pictures of Sri Sri, of Guruji! Look at him playing bat and ball when he was a kid! Look at this picture! He is wearing shorts and is cycling.'

The world spun around me. I was in the Santa Monica office of the founder of Clearstone Venture Partners, the firm that had given me eighteen crore rupees to start a gaming business, and this very person was showing me pictures of my guru that no one had seen before!

Bill noticed the awe and shock on my face, smiled and said, 'Alok, Guruji and I go back a long way. We have lots to discuss.'

As we walked back to the party, just before going our separate ways, Bill looked at me seriously and asked, 'Alok, hasn't Guruji told you about drinking? Each glass of wine is worth forty days of sadhana (spiritual practice)! Don't squander your sadhana away...'

I was speechless.

A few minutes later, while I was trying to collect my thoughts, a smartly dressed, tall, athletic Indian man came up to me and said, 'Alok, where have you been hiding? I've been looking for you!'

I instantly recognised Sumant Mandal whom I had met in Mumbai. Rahul worked with Sumant who was a Partner of Clearstone, based in LA. They both were responsible for the India business. I instantly warmed up to Sumant and excitedly narrated the details of my meeting with Bill Elkus. Sumant grinned and said, 'Ah, It's nice you figured out how to meet the most important man in the company! You're a smart entrepreneur.'

Of course, Sumant meant the remark as a joke, but I couldn't help thinking how accurately he had described the significance of my meeting. Funnily, I had done nothing smart to meet Bill in the first place.

As I hung out with Sumant, he told me, 'Alok, Bill and my father-in-law know Sri Sri from a long time. They all are good friends and closely connected.'

As I heard this, my mind went into a tizzy once again. I wondered who Sumant's father-in-law was who knew Sri Sri so well. Sumant lived in the US, and while I knew that Sri Sri had many American followers, I was curious to find out who this person was. I cleared my throat and calmly asked Sumant, 'Who is your father-in-law?'

Sumant replied, 'Deepak Chopra.'

The minute I heard the name Deepak Chopra, everything lit up around me. Instantly I understood the connection. Deepak Chopra and Sri Sri were the two favourite disciples of the great spiritual guru Maharishi Mahesh Yogi—the inventor of Transcendental Meditation (TM), the guru of the Beatles and many other celebrities. Sri Sri and Deepak Chopra were 'Guru Bhais' (disciples of the same guru).

I realised that it was beyond ordinary coincidence that Sumant and Bill—two of the most influential people I would be working with for the next decade—had a direct connection to my guru and his lineage. I later found out that the third partner—Jim Armstrong, who was very helpful and supportive of Games2win—was also very close to Sri Sri.

It seemed that the universe was in charge of the situation, and I was simply following the path it had laid out for me. My chance meeting with Rahul Khanna at the ISB wasn't a coincidence at all. It was all part of a perfectly orchestrated divine plan to get me closer to the people I had a deep karmic connection with, and who would also help me build my business.

Connecting the Dots

The universe keeps sending life-changing opportunities our way. It is the benevolent nature of the universe. When we need to make a gigantic, positive leap forward, unseen energies change the circumstances around us, so that we can take that chance. All that we need to do is to be alert, open-minded and willing to accept such magically curated events and take advantage of them.

Exercise

Close your eyes and think of the times and situations when you found yourself in the right place, at the right time and met the right people. Do you get a sense that a higher power had been your ally and friend all along? Cherish those moments and feel grateful for them. Appreciate and accept the power of forces you cannot fathom so that you are attuned to receiving their gifts and blessings. Don't have a closed mind and falsely think that you are in control of all the events in your life. Quieten your logical mind and accept that there are some things you will neither understand nor need to. That way, you will quickly be blessed with the divine magic meant for you.

THE TALE OF TWO CUPS

The Blue Cup

In 2009, a couple of years after my first trip to Clearstone's Santa Monica office, Sumant invited me to the firm's Annual Day. At that event, the CEOs of Clearstone's portfolio companies met and discussed business, markets, trends and ideas. The venue was the swanky Ritz Carlton Hotel at Marina Del Rey in LA, near Santa Monica.

Clearstone has the distinction of funding several of the early and super-successful startups of the US such as mp3.com, PayPal and Overture. Some of the legendary entrepreneurs of those companies were also attending the meeting. At the venue, I distinctly remember meeting a shy, soft-spoken man who listened intently to the description of my gaming startup. After my long spiel, when I asked him what he did, he gently said, 'I founded mp3.com. Have you heard of it?' Instantly I was struck by the utmost humility of Michael Roberston and made a mental note to myself to talk less and listen more.

After the long sessions of the day concluded, the Clearstone team sprung a huge surprise when they announced that Deepak Chopra was in the house as their special guest! All of us eagerly sat in a large ballroom and waited for him to arrive.

A few minutes later, Deepak arrived and greeted everyone. He looked around, picked up a blue cup, held it high in the air, and asked the audience, 'Can someone tell me the colour of this cup?'

Almost immediately, a man in the front row said, 'It's blue.'

What Deepak Chopra said next was so profound that it changed my life.

He said, 'Let's understand how we all saw the blue cup. First, rays of light fell on the cup and reflected in the direction of your eyes. Next, when they reached your eyes, the light rays entered via your iris, travelled through your cornea, and rested on your retina. When I asked, "What colour is the cup?", your brain started its work to answer my question. Your retina processed the information and transmitted its knowledge to your mind. Your brain motivated your lips to speak the word, "blue". You then said, "It's blue".'

Deepak paused and asked, 'Does everyone agree with my narration and sequence of events?'

We all unanimously agreed with him.

He took a long pause and said, 'Each event that I described was separate from the other. Each event took its own time to be completed, no matter how small or minuscule that might have been. And, the events happened in a sequence.'

Deepak paused again and said, 'If you minutely examine

any sequence of events, there will always be a gap between them. That gap, however small, always exists.'

Slowing down his pace, Deepak said, 'By practising regular meditation, you can develop the ability to spot gaps between your thoughts, which are nothing but events. At first, it may seem impossible, but with regular practice, you will develop that skill. When you reach this meditative state, you will experience super-alertness. As your practice gets deeper, your awareness will expand greatly and align itself with the universal consciousness. Then, your desires and needs will easily get fulfilled. Please meditate regularly to find gaps between your thoughts and cultivate a mind of super-consciousness and alertness.'

As I heard the last words, I was utterly mesmerised. No one had ever explained the concept of meditation to me in such lucid and profound terms. I had goosebumps as I thought of the gaps between my thoughts. Just as Deepak was leaving, Sumant introduced him to me, and later, we exchanged emails. I could not believe that I was corresponding with Deepak Chopra just a few minutes after I had met him for the first time. Then again, I remembered my guru Sri Sri Ravishankar, and his guru, Maharishi Mahesh Yogi. It only seemed natural that I should have met Deepak Chopra. We were all Guru Bhais, after all. And among Guru Bhais, anything was possible.

As I left California, the blue cup appeared in my mind. I wondered, 'Where would I find my own blue cup? Who would give it to me? What purpose would it serve me?'

Your Cup Is Full. Empty Your Cup.

Two years after my meeting with Deepak Chopra, I was quietly sitting on my blue spongy yoga mat in Mumbai. It was a Sunday, the day I practised the 'Long Sudarshan Kriya'. The Long Kriya is a deeper and more intense version of the regular Sudarshan Kriya that I had learned almost ten years ago, in 2001. I had practised my Kriya every day, without a break. The Kriya had transformed me and made me calm, composed, intuitive and super-creative. I attributed surviving the harsh and cruel dotcom bust partially to my spiritual practices. The Kriya was the cornerstone of my meditations. Thanks to it, I was happy, successful and focused.

However, deep down, inside of me, something was missing. Even though I had tasted decent success as a digital entrepreneur and found my fair share of fame and glory, I felt incomplete and unaccomplished, and felt as if I was still struggling. The feeling of incompleteness kept surfacing inside me.

After the Long Kriya session was over, I went up to Nikita Inamdar, the Art of Living teacher who was supervising the practice, and told her, 'Nikita, something is wrong. I don't feel enthusiastic nowadays. Even though I do my Kriya every day, I feel nothing has changed. I don't get a kick or a high anymore. Can you tell me what's going wrong? What am I missing?'

Nikita is one of the most accomplished teachers of the Art of Living. She looked at me, gently smiled and almost reflexively, without hesitating, said, 'Alok, your cup is full. Empty your cup.'

A shiver ran down my spine when I heard the word 'cup'. Deepak Chopra and his narration of the blue cup story flashed in front of me. I said, 'Nikita, please explain. What cup do I need to empty? What you just said has gone way above my head!'

Nikita gently replied, 'Alok, you have received everything you wanted in your life and more. Your cup of life is full. Now, you need to empty your cup to feel thirsty again. Only when you are thirsty will you feel enjoyment in quenching your thirst. How can you empty your cup? By giving, sharing and helping others. Only when you become empty will you feel like filling yourself again.'

I had tears in my eyes when Nikita said these words to me. I felt as if a heavy dark veil had lifted from my eyes. I had just received an understanding of my own cup. Now, all I had to do was to empty it.

That same week, almost impulsively, without thinking too much, I began to donate money, clothes and medicines. I visited hospitals and abandoned children's homes to find ways to help the people there. Yet, nothing shifted inside of me. I felt no change in fulfilment. On the contrary, visiting old-age homes and seeing abandoned children made me feel depressed and sad. This experiment did not work for me.

I thought about my feelings and remembered what Deepak Chopra had said. He had recommended that we meditate, observe our thoughts and try and spot the gaps between them. I knew I had to be super-mindful to find my own cup and the source of my higher happiness.

A few weeks after practising daily meditation, I received my answer, in the form of a question! I asked myself, 'Alok, what is the one thing you have, which is the most precious of them all? What has taken you the longest to acquire? What could be the best gift you could give someone?'

The insight came like a flash of lightning. I realised that the most precious thing I owned was my in-depth and extensive knowledge of entrepreneurship and starting up businesses which I had gained over years of building, selling and funding startups. I instinctively realised that if I shared those experiences and learnings, I would help a lot of people who had no access to such insights anywhere else.

Almost immediately after, I started blogging and called myself 'Rodinhood'. I felt inspired by Augustin Rodin's sculpture 'The Thinker', and the legend of Robin Hood. So I combined 'Thinking and Giving' and called myself Rodinhood.

Three years later, I had published over two hundred blogs that were very well-received. My columns appeared in the *Economic Times of India, Wall Street Journal* (online version) and other popular publications. Thanks to my writings, I was invited to speak at Harvard Business School and the Wharton Business School. I went further and established 'Therodinhoods'—a social media community of entrepreneurs who would collectively write, share and meet to help each other and the community. Therodinhoods swelled to over ten thousand in number, and we held over fifty events in over twenty cities. In 2018, I successfully published my first book *Why I Stopped wearing my Socks* which comprised my best startup, business and personal life experiences and lessons. That book became a bestseller on Amazon India and also won the C.K. Prahalad Best Business Book Award for 2019.

When I think back, not a day has passed since I published my first blog when I haven't received a message from someone thanking me for something I have written that has helped them.

I managed to do something meaningful to help people. My lack of sharing and giving was my gap that Nikita had inspired me to see. And as she had predicted, a few weeks after I had started to write and share, I began to feel a change in my energy and mood. I experienced a deep sense of fulfilment by helping others. I had found my 'cup' and even managed to fill and empty it several times.

Connecting the Dots

Seek mentors and personal guides. Your personal growth can be ignited when you meet wise people who can give you life-changing insights. It is also critical to find deep fulfilment in your work and personal life. In this context, my guru Sri Sri Ravishankar once shared a profound knowledge point about the 'quality of happiness'. He asks that we compare the different sources of happiness by measuring how long the joy they provide lasts. For instance, a good meal can give us pleasure that lasts for a couple of hours. Alcohol provides happiness for an evening. Cigarettes deliver joy that lasts for a few minutes. When you exercise, your elevated state of mind lasts for a day. So, what is that activity that delivers the happiness that lasts for a long, long time? For me, it is the happiness I get when I serve people.

If you have helped people in the past, you would probably agree with me. If you haven't, you must give it a try!

Exercise

After reading this, contemplate and do a few random acts of kindness. Do something beyond giving food or money to those you know. How about calling someone you've fallen out with and surprising them with your call? Or going out of your way and assisting someone who needs your help and support?

After your good deeds, reflect on how you feel. Judge the happiness quality of these actions vis-a-vis from the other regular sources from which you have derived happiness in the past. If you have found a newer and higher form of joy, indulge in it more often!

THE CAVE

My Nana gifted me a copy of *Autobiography of a Yogi* when I was fifteen years old. I remember it had the stamp of 'A.H. Wheeler' printed inside. A.H. Wheeler is a legacy bookseller whose book carts and stores are ubiquitous at many Indian railway stations and platforms. My Nana probably bought the book while on a train journey.

Autobiography of a Yogi is a fascinating read. When Walter Issacson released his seminal biography, *Steve Jobs*, the world learned how much Steve Jobs, the founder of Apple, loved *Autobiography of a Yogi*. It was the only book Jobs downloaded on his iPad and read every year. It was also the gift Steve Jobs left instructions for to be given away at his funeral.

The book is about Paramhansa Yogananda, a renowned Indian spiritual master, who spent many years in the US spreading the knowledge of spirituality and teaching Kriya Yoga—an ancient meditation practice that had been kept secret for centuries. The book traces Paramhansa's life and the incredible people he met, as he travelled the world. Every chapter in the book is an epic story.

I read the book as an impressionable teenager and was instantly captivated by it. The stories of spiritual masters and the miracles they performed were profoundly engaging and mystical. I believed the tales to be real and deeply longed to meet the people mentioned in them. While the book's contents were gripping, there was a particular picture in the book—a photograph of the saint Lahiri Mahasaya—that I adored the most. It was a black-and-white image of Lahiri Mahasaya captured sitting cross-legged, with a half-smile and drooping eyes. He was in a state of complete bliss—in samadhi. The moment I saw it, I was spellbound. For years, I would go back to the book just to stare at Lahiri Mahasaya's smile, because he looked naughty to me! Strangely, I became very fond of Lahiri Mahasaya, thanks to this photograph.

In the book, there is also the mention of a Himalayan cave that Lahiri Mahasaya chances upon while trekking in the hilly regions of Ranikhet—a hill station located in the state of Uttarakhand. The saint describes how he first met the immortal, deathless saint Babaji (Mahavatar Babaji) near the cave, and his incredible experiences with him. The chapters in the book based on Lahiri Mahasaya's adventures in and around the cave are simply magical.

Sometime in September 2011, I noticed an advertisement on Facebook to 'Visit Babaji's Cave'. When I reread the ad, I recalled the story of this cave from the book. I was amazed that the same cave still existed and that there was even a tour that took people to it!

The ad led me to Ananda Sangha—a global spiritual organisation founded by Swami Kriyananda, a direct disciple of Paramhansa Yogananda. Ananda Sangha has a base in India, and their Delhi centre was the organiser of this cave trip. After quickly checking the itinerary details, I signed up for the trip scheduled for early November of that same year.

In the evening, I told Chhavi about my travel plan. While Chhavi had done the Art of Living course a year after me and practised her Sudarshan Kriya regularly, she wasn't interested in going to the cave and she didn't bother asking me too many questions about it.

One week before the trip, Chhavi told me one morning, 'Alok, I want to come with you to the cave. Please find out if that's possible.' (Even today, Chhavi tells me that she cannot explain why she changed her mind. It's one of the most puzzling incidents in her life). I checked with Daya and Keshava—the fantastic couple who managed Ananda Sangha, Delhi—if she could accompany me. They confirmed that there was just one place left. Chhavi signed up, too!

A few days later, we were on the way. We travelled from Delhi to Kathgodam by train, and further by bus to Ranikhet. Along the way, we visited Neem Karoli Baba's Ashram (about which you will read a few chapters later). In the early evening, we checked into a cosy hotel in Ranikhet. The resort overlooked the Himalayas, and we could spot famous mountains such as Nanda Devi and Trisul from our room balconies! I had never visited Ranikhet before. That day I understood why it was called Rani (queen) Khet (field). This place was majestic and throbbed with divine energy.

Early the next morning, we boarded a bus that drove us to the Dronagiri mountain range from where we could trek up to the cave. Sixty other pilgrims accompanied us. The drive would take two-and-a-half hours.

In the bus, Keshava read passages from *Autobiography of a Yogi*. He wanted to familiarise the pilgrims with the cave and the events that happened there. As Keshava read, he came to the passage when Lahiri Mahasaya found himself lost on Dronagiri mountain (the mountain we were travelling to). While trying to find his way, the saint was stunned to hear someone calling out his name. As he continued climbing the steep path, he saw a handsome young lad, standing on a rocky ledge, beckoning him towards a cave. The lad was none other than the mystical Babaji! What Keshava read next sent shivers down my spine. As Lahiri looked at the young boy, he was amazed to notice that Babaji looked just like himself. In Lahiri's own words, 'I noticed with astonishment that, except for his copper-coloured hair, he bore a remarkable resemblance to myself.'

When I heard these words, I wondered how could Babaji look like Lahiri Mahasaya when there was no direct connection between them? I knew how Babaji looked and I had also seen Lahiri Mahasaya's photo. Surely, there was no resemblance between the two. This puzzle haunted me for a long time until I had my own realisation about its meaning, a few weeks later.

After driving for another forty-five minutes, we reached a milestone that read 'Dronagiri'. At this point, we alighted from the bus and began our trek up the mountain. The path was probably the same one Lahiri Mahasaya had trod on before encountering Babaji. After a vigorous climb that lasted for almost an hour, we reached the rocky ledge that led to the cave. Unlike what I had imagined it to be, it was small and compact, not large and deep as I had assumed it was. The pilgrims settled down and took turns to meditate inside. The cave could accommodate about ten people at a time.

When my turn came, I chanced to be seated near the cave's entrance. It was a beautiful, bright and sunny November afternoon. The birds chirped all around us. I felt so blessed. Never had I imagined that I would be sitting to meditate in a real Himalayan cave and that, too, a cave as blessed as this one!

I closed my eyes and slowly slipped into meditation. A few minutes passed, and my mind began to quieten down. I was completely relaxed. Then, everything changed around me. It felt like winter. In my mind's eye, I could see snowflakes falling outside, and tree branches covered with fluffy white snow. I heard wild animals lurking outside. For many minutes, everything around me felt so real. My mind began to wonder. Had I visited this cave earlier, sometime before? How else could I visualise it so well, that, too, in the cold white winter months?

I have no recollection of how much time passed until the active buzzing of a bumblebee brought me back to my reality. Through my closed eyes, I sensed the bright sunlight outside and heard the birds chirping again. I continued to meditate silently for a few minutes more, then gently opened my eyes, acclimatised myself to my surroundings and exited the cave.

When all the pilgrims had completed their meditation, we trekked back to our waiting bus and then drove back to Ranikhet. The winter sensation I experienced in the cave seemed so surreal to me that I didn't mention it to anyone. Maybe, I didn't quite believe it myself.

Two days later, Chhavi and I were back in Mumbai. We realised that something had changed within us. Unbelievable as it may sound, we both began missing the cave so much that we wanted to go back to it. As if in complete sync, we started to think of Babaji all the time. He kept flooding our thoughts, meditations and conversations. I wondered, how could this have happened? I felt deeply conflicted. Was I disloyal? For eleven years, Sri Sri had been my guru, guide and spiritual mentor. Now, all I could think of was Babaji? How was I supposed to resolve this conflict of my spiritual loyalty? I spent many days and nights disturbed by these thoughts. Finally, I decided to find the answer via sincere meditation. And the answer did come! I realised that Sri Sri was my Guru and Babaji was my God. Guru and God had always co-existed in the lives of spiritual seekers, and I was fortunate enough to have found both of them.

One late evening, as I was flipping through *Autobiography of a Yogi*, I checked out my favourite photograph of Lahiri Mahasaya, with his mischievous grin. When I saw the picture, my heart skipped many beats. I instantly recalled the story Keshava had read out in the bus describing Lahiri Mahasaya's meeting with Babaji. Lahiri Mahasaya had said, 'I noticed with astonishment that, except for his copper-coloured hair, he bore a remarkable resemblance to myself.'

That very instant, I realised why I had found that picture of Lahiri Mahasaya so endearing for all these years. As I studied the picture carefully, it became clear that Lahiri Mahasaya did look like Babaji, albeit an older version. A very young Lahiri Mahasaya would have looked just like Babaji. And that is when the final realisation dawned on me. I had felt deeply attracted to Lahiri Mahsaya's picture because he looked like Babaji, even without my realising it. I was actually in love with Babaji from the very beginning. It was Babaji whom I would go back to look at in the book. The trip to the cave and the story of Lahiri Mahasaya meeting Babaji made it all to clear to me. I had goosebumps all over, and waves of love and gratitude swept over me.

Just as Babaji had invited Lahiri Mahasaya to come to His Cave on Dronagiri mountain, so also, Babaji had invited Chhavi and me to visit Him and meditate in His Cave. This was the Cave in which Babaji had initiated Lahiri Mahasaya into the ancient technique of Kriya Yoga and brought back memories of his past life. It was here that Lahiri Mahasaya had meditated for years at end. This was the Cave that had witnessed the divine love of the Supreme Guru Babaji and his disciple, Lahiri Mahasaya. This was no ordinary Cave. It was a magical, divine Cave infused with the immortal vibrations of Babaji, and the birth place of the modern Kriya Yoga revolution.

Babaji had made both of us his followers, and we would soon find out that our lives would never be the same again.

Connecting the Dots

Places of worship and the homes and habitations of accomplished spiritual practitioners have high levels of positive energy concentrations. Nature itself is a great uplifter. When we visit such places, we attain the ability to go deeper within ourselves and achieve a high quality of mindfulness and meditation. We have deep connections with places, people and situations that may seem puzzling at first but which reveal themselves to us at the right time. We must be open to such ideas and concepts and not have mental blocks about them.

Exercise

Close your eyes, and try and remember if you have experienced familiarity with people and places? Did you find out what attracted you to them? Haven't you felt instantly peaceful and relaxed in areas of worship or when you are amidst pure, beautiful nature? Resolve to be open-minded and mindful of such circumstances. Often, they are the windows to life-changing experiences and upliftments. Accept that everything doesn't have to be scientific. Sometimes, fuzzy things can be right for you!

PARKING FRENZY

After I returned to Mumbai, I read *Autobiography of a Yogi* all over again. Amongst the great saints mentioned in it, Babaji emerged as my absolute favourite. Babaji is a deathless master who has assisted many of the world's great sages, whenever they have appeared on earth. He has mentored them on their path to enlightenment. Babaji's title 'Mahavatar' means that he is a great avatar, who remains alive by his own will, to spread the secret knowledge of spiritual liberation.

The first, immediate change Chhavi and I experienced after we returned from the Cave was the igniting of intense affection for our guru, Sri Sri Ravishankar. Almost intuitively, Chhavi and I began doing everything possible to serve Guruji. I conducted social media programmes, workshops and entrepreneurship sessions at the Art of Living Ashram in Bangalore. To become better practitioners, we enrolled in higher level Art of Living courses that we had postponed all these years. Chhavi believes that the trip to the Cave was her moment of great transformation. An easy-going spiritual seeker who would take each day as it came, the Cave got Chhavi supercharged. She completed advanced spiritual courses and eventually became an Art of Living teacher. A year later, I followed her and became an Art of Living teacher myself. Both of us started teaching the first level course.

An astonishing aspect of Babaji is his immortality. He has lived for centuries in his body form and will continue to do so until his work is complete. He is omnipresent and omniscient. As described in *Autobiography of a Yogi*, Babaji comes to his followers when they need him. Just '… remembering Babaji's name with a pure heart invokes an instant spiritual blessing', Lahiri Mahasaya is quoted as saying in the book. As the days progressed, I began remembering Babaji many times a day. With the innocence of a child, I would plead with him to grant me at least one darshan (appearance).

While Babaji and our spiritual progress became our new joy, the mundane aspects of our lives continued as usual. My mobile gaming startup Games2win became a challenging business that required me to put in long hours and continuously innovate. Our two daughters were in school, and Chhavi worked hard as a product manager at Games2win and a patient mom at home. Juggling work, spirituality, parenting and home chores became very demanding for Chhavi and me.

Amidst this challenging routine, an unexpected irritant emerged. The apartment complex in Mumbai where we lived, decided to paint the residents' car garages stark white. The buildings' old garages were designed for the older generation of cars such as Fiats and Ambassadors. New age cars occupy much more space. Parking my car in a small garage was always a tough task, especially in reverse mode. The day after my garage's repainting, my parking problems peaked. I was blinded by the fresh white paint that reflected in my car's parking camera. I knew I would damage my car if I didn't do something to remedy the problem immediately.

One morning, I chanced upon the painter who was still working in the building and instructed him to paint a big black X mark in the centre of my garage wall. It would break the monotony of the stark white walls and help me park. I could even focus on it while reversing. That same evening, as per my instructions, a large black X came up on my wall. It looked quite ugly and sinister, considering that all the other garage walls had no markings at all. The next day, when our soft-spoken and gentle building secretary Mr Patel noticed my X, he politely came up to me and said, 'Alok Bhai, can't you paint something better than this mark? I am sure you can think of some better ideas?' I nodded in embarrassment and spontaneously told the painter to remove the X and write the acronym OBO (Om Babaji Om) on the garage wall. There could be no better marking than that, I thought, and I would remember Babaji even while parking my car!

Everything settled down, but my restlessness to experience Babaji kept growing. If Babaji came to those devotees who sincerely called him, then surely I deserved to meet him, too! As the days passed, I started going crazy about Babaji. In my meditations, I told him, 'Babaji, I have no clue where you are. You supposedly roam the universe but spare no time for me. I am crazy about you and yet there is no sign of you or even an acknowledgement from your side. How do I know you are for real? How can I experience you? Oh Babaji, do something that signals to me that you know I exist. You're the Mahavatar. *Do something spectacular, something insane for me!'* Like a child throwing tantrums and demanding gifts from his parents, here I was, kicking up a massive fuss for tricks and treats from Babaji.

A couple of years before my visit to the Cave, my mobile startup Games2win had begun publishing mobile games. Before that, we operated as an online gaming website, producing games for web browsers. Making mobile games was a completely different business. We had assumed that replicating our online games as mobile games would be the solution, but that was an ill-conceived business plan. The first lot of mobile games we made were tacky and clumsy. If we had to succeed in mobile games, we would have to start from scratch. It was an uphill task and we were working on it, but were yet to make a dent.

Six months had passed since my Cave visit. I was hounding Babaji in my prayers every day, but there was no sign of him. I had not experienced any Babaji magic, yet!

The only minor excitement was the OBO mark in my garage. A few building residents came up to ask me what it meant. I told them it was an abbreviation for Om Babaji Om. But none of them understood. They let it be and never asked me for more details.

On a Monday in the first week of June, as I walked into the office, Dinu (my colleague who I had dragged to LA), came up and said, 'Alok, I want to tell you that something unusual is happening. We had released a game called

"Parking Frenzy" on the iTunes store a few weeks ago, and it was completely flat in terms of downloads. Now, there seems to be some movement on it.'

I ignored Dinesh's excitement. I knew Parking Frenzy well. Just before the game's release, I had a showdown with the team members (including Dinu) for the poor art they had used in the game, which looked more retro than modern. Even though the gameplay was fun, it looked and felt like it was from the clumsy Eighties.

In the afternoon, Dinesh met me again and said, 'Alok, we need your attention now. The Parking Frenzy game is showing massive activity.'

This time, I paid heed to Dinesh's request. As I scanned the game's online analytics, I was amazed to notice a massive spike in downloads. When I looked up Parking Frenzy on social media, I was stunned to find thousands of teen girls in the US tweeting about the game! We had not promoted or advertised the game. There had been no PR or any topical event that could have brought attention to the game. This activity was completely unusual.

Since the game was scaling very fast, I decided to test it thoroughly, to check if everything was working fine. While playing it, I was dismayed to notice that many of the advertising units in it were not working perfectly. If this game was going to blow up in terms of popularity, I needed to mend it fast, so that we could monetise it effectively. After getting my team to get the ad units fixed, I emailed Apple and told them about our urgency to update the game. (There is a unique email ID on which you can email Apple for such emergencies, restricted to usage once a year. I decided to use my yearly quota for this game.) Apple responded favourably and fast-tracked our request. Our new Parking Frenzy game was updated and made live on the iTunes app store in less than two days, as opposed to the normal process that usually would have taken anywhere between seven to ten days.

The next three days became a blur for me and everyone in the company. Every hour, as we would refresh our browsers to check the top app rankings of the world, Parking Frenzy would show a massive upward spike. The game continued climbing the ranks in the racing and games categories in most iTunes markets. It became the number one game in the UK and in several other leading countries in the world.

At 1 a.m. (IST) on 12 June 2012, Parking Frenzy became the number one game and the number one app in the US iTunes store and other top app stores in the world. Social media in the US had exploded, and teen girls were going crazy playing the game and writing stories about how this game was helping them become better drivers. They were posting pictures of the game and tagging their friends, urging them to download the game. Till then, no game from India had ever become the number one game in the US iTunes store, leave alone the number one app. (That record stands to this date). What happened with Parking Frenzy was unbelievable. In my heart, I could not understand the success of the game. Nothing made sense to me. In my opinion, the game was ordinary and tacky.

But its spectacular success made me mail my investors and broadcast the news on my social media. Congratulations began to flood in from everywhere!

Late that night, I drove home, exhausted, but super-excited. It had been one of the best days of my life. Never in my dreams had I imagined owning the number one game on the iTunes stores worldwide. When I neared my garage, I began to reverse my car. As I looked at the parking assist screen, I saw 'OBO' staring at me, emblazoned on the white wall. My gaze became transfixed at those alphabets, and I braked hard. I began trembling and had goosebumps all over. Instantly, I connected everything. I was parking a car, and Babaji (OBO) was guiding me. My game Parking Frenzy was about parking cars, too. Parking Frenzy's inexplicable and unbelievable success was Babaji's doing!

That day, I realised the power and presence of Babaji. I had begged him to do something 'insane' for me, and this is how he had responded! He had made my wildest dream come true and given me a clear signal of his magic. Even today, when I show people the graphs and downloads trajectory of the Parking Frenzy game, they refuse to believe that it was wholly organic and viral. They tell me that no parking game has ever hit the number one slot on the US iTunes charts and that I must have done lots of secret and expensive marketing to achieve that rank! Of course, I know the secret of the success of the game, but dare not explain t to the naysayers.

Parking Frenzy amassed ten million downloads that week itself. The game paved the way for Games2win to dominate the car parking and driving games genre on the app stores in the years to come. My company won instant global recognition, and my investors were delighted to own equity in a company that had delivered a global number one game from India—something no one had done before.

Connecting the Dots

Crazy things happen when you wish for them. We should never place restrictions on our ambitions and hearts' desires. The world of successful people is full of stories of how they hoped for impossible outcomes. My firm view is that the universe is always in listening mode. If you want something badly and put out your heart to achieve it, it will manifest. The Gods and Gurus are often the channel for such prayers to be answered. They are not magicians, but enablers of the higher powers to help those in need. When someone asked Sai Baba of Shirdi why he regularly produced miracles for his devotees, he replied, 'I give them what they want so that they want what I give.' In essence, he was satiating the smaller wants of his devotees so that they would be prepared to receive his higher blessings.

Exercise

Close your eyes and take a few deep breaths. Think of something you have always wanted but never received. Make a heartfelt wish for it. If you have a god or guru, keep them in your prayer. Then leave it to the universe to grant you your request. Don't crave for it anymore. Stay assured that if whatever you have asked for is indeed right for you, it will come to you, at the right place and time.

THE INCIDENT AT THIKSEY MONASTERY

When I was in school, I read Leo Tolstoy's short story 'The Imp and the Crust'. It is the story of what alcohol can do to a good man. That story stayed with me as I grew up. I vowed never to drink in my life. When Chhavi married me, she had never tasted a drink in her life. My grandparents, with whom I lived, neither drank nor endorsed alcohol. Chhavi and I made friends with people who were complete teetotallers. All this meant that drinking was out of the question for me. Or so I thought.

When I became an internet entrepreneur, everything changed. In my early startup days, I attended business events, social parties and conferences and thrived on extensive networking. Soon, I gave in to enjoying alcoholic cocktails. During that same time, I met Rajiv Samant, who had just launched Sula wines in India. I signed up for his first wine tasting class and began appreciating wines. A year later, a dear friend, Sulakshna Pathak, who headed marketing for the Moet Hennessy group in India invited me to her signature cognac tasting sessions. By the time I turned thirty-two, I knew more about wines and malts than most experts, including my father (who had always enjoyed his fine single malts and whiskeys). Thankfully, alcohol never became a problem or an addiction for me. I just liked to enjoy my occasional drink and the merry feeling that came along with it.

In May 2012, Daya and Keshava—our Ananda Sangha friends who had organised our trip to Babaji's Cave—announced a meditation trip to Leh, in Ladakh. Their itinerary promised a visit to ten of the most ancient monasteries in the region. Chhavi and I signed up instantly. After our visit to the Cave, we had grown to love visiting spiritual places, and when such opportunities presented themselves, we quickly grabbed them.

As a principle, alcohol does not mix well with spirituality. When you taste the intoxication of the divine, artificial replacements seem redundant. I had begun to experience this. Since my trip to the Cave, my alcohol consumption had dropped. All of a sudden, I was not able to consume more than two drinks, considerably lower than the four drinks I had earlier. Also, after an evening of light drinking, I would invariably wake up with a bad headache the following morning. Intuitively, I understood that I had to drop alcohol. Yet, despite the discomfort and the visible signs, I could not stay away from a few drinks at parties and celebrations. My inability to drop alcohol began to bother me.

As we began our trip to Ladakh, I wished from deep inside my heart to get rid of my drinking habit.

After landing in Leh, our pilgrims' group checked into a comfortable hotel and made it our residential base. Over the next few days, we visited some of the most ancient and historic monasteries in the region. Even though we were visiting Leh in May, the temperature outside was usually zero degrees. Our group would travel to monasteries by bus and spend the day meditating there.

On the fourth day of the trip, as we gathered for dinner, Keshava announced, 'Tomorrow is a uniquely special day. It will be Buddha Purnima (Buddha's birthday), and we will be celebrating it in the land of Buddha. Just before dawn, we will leave for a special meditation arranged for us. Please don't be late.' Even though no more details were forthcoming, all of us were excited! We knew we were in for a special treat.

The next morning, in freezing temperatures and total darkness, we quietly boarded our bus that took us to Thiksey monastery. Thiksey is one of the oldest and most beautiful monasteries in Ladakh. For me, the main attraction of Thiksey is the statue of the Maitreya Buddha, which is two storeys tall. He looks amazingly spectacular and royal. And, I am not the only one who is in awe of this Buddha statue. In the corner of the second floor room of Thiksey's Buddha, there is a letter from the Dalai Lama that reads, 'I have travelled far and wide and seen many Buddhas, but yours is truly beautiful.'

After reaching the monastery grounds, we began settling down in the assembly hall to meditate. Keshava had arranged for our group to sit inside the main hall, not usually available for visitors. As the monks began to filter in for the morning chanting, Keshava whispered to us, 'Just let their chanting wash over your chakras (energy points in the body). Until the chanting gets over, don't get up.'

If you have heard Buddhist monastery chanting before, you would recognise how uplifting it can be. Even though it is guttural in sound, if you focus on its energy, a deep feeling of cleansing and fulfilment begins to manifest as the chants get recited repeatedly.

As the Thiksey monastery monks began to chant, I slipped into a deep meditation. Their chanting gently wafted into my ears and travelled to every cell in my body. All along, while the ceremony continued, I sat completely still. I wanted to honour and respect this holy process with all my attention and focus. An hour later, I was disturbed by a slight movement next to me. I opened my eyes slightly and noticed Chhavi and a few pilgrims getting up and moving out of the hall. As I watched them, I remembered Keshava's instruction to 'not get up or leave'. So, I closed my eyes and went back to my meditation. About thirty minutes later, the chanting ended. For many minutes, even though the monks had stopped their recitations, I could still hear their singing in my ears. A while later, taking our own time and slowly becoming aware of our surroundings, Keshava and I got up, bowed to the monks and the holy Buddhas and exited the hall. We leisurely walked across the ancient courtyard and met the rest of the pilgrims in the restaurant area, at the entrance of the monastery, and later headed back to the bus.

Towards the end of the day, my spiritual mentor Daya caught up with me and asked, 'Alok, how is your drinking going? How's that working for you?' I was a bit taken aback by the question. How did Daya know I was so bothered with my drinking? Could she read it in my eyes? Was Daya blessed with special intuitive powers I had failed to notice?

I looked at Daya and shyly said, 'Daya, I continue to drink. I want to stop but don't know how to. I don't seem to be able to muster up the will power to quit drinking.' Daya looked at me with a gentle smile and compassionately said, 'Alok, you will have to think about it. If you have to tread the spiritual path, you will have to work on it...' I smiled at her and let the discussion rest. Neither of us raised the topic again.

Chhavi and I returned to Mumbai the day after. We were exhausted by the strenuous travel and fell into a deep sleep the moment we hit our bed.

I awoke early the next morning and decided to meditate. In preparation, I opened my cupboard to retrieve my blue-coloured silk meditation asana (soft mat). As I bent down to collect it, I noticed most of my single malts and whiskeys neatly stacked in the corner. For some strange reason, I kept staring at the bottles. Then, a bizarre thought crossed my mind. I asked myself, 'What are these bottles doing here? Do I need them?' It was a very surreal moment. It felt as if I had never seen those bottles before and wondered how they got there.

I composed myself and sat down to meditate. Forty minutes later, when my session ended, I opened my cupboard and cleared the shelves of all the alcohol bottles stocked inside. I got them packed and took them to the office. In the evening, I asked my colleagues to help themselves to any of the liquor they liked (a decision I regret today.) I also called up my father and offered him some of the unopened bottles I had in stock. He was thrilled to receive them from me.

On that magical day, the memory of alcohol vanished from my mind. Overnight, I could not remember the drinks I used to enjoy so much. The desire to unwind with a drink in my hand seemed as if it had never existed. Instead of me leaving alcohol, alcohol left me.

In retrospect, how I wish I would have simply destroyed all those bottles instead. If alcohol had bothered me and made me feel compromised, what business did I have distributing it amongst those whom I cared for? Just to avoid wasting this expensive hoard of mine, I was willingly harming people. This incident taught me a powerful lesson to deal with selfish behaviour. The moral lesson I relearned was the biblical commandment—'Do unto others as you would have them do unto you'.

Over the next few weeks, I realised that such a significant personal change did not happen on its own. Leaving addictive habits is one of the hardest battles human beings have ever fought. In my case, I had forgotten my experience of drinking alcohol all together. When I retraced the events leading to the miracle, it became clear to me. The powerful and divine chanting of holy monks at Thiksey monastery had cleansed me of my addiction. As Keshava had said, 'Let the mantras wash your chakras.' I had gone to Thiskey with a heavy heart and had returned light, unburdened and free of regrets.

That was surely a sign of my spiritual blossoming.

Connecting the Dots

Paramhansa Yogananda said, 'Chanting is half the battle won.' My guru Sri Sri often reiterates, 'If you chant Om Namah Shivaya every day, you will no longer be bothered by constellation problems and astrological prophecies.' Chanting is simply reciting and repeating spiritual words rhythmically. These words have deep vibrations that get unlocked to benefit both the person reciting and the persons listening. Buddhist chanting has become a global phenomenon precisely for this reason.

Exercise

I would strongly recommend that you chant every day. You can try some mantras and choose the one that suits you the most. Then, make it a point to recite it for at least twenty minutes every day. You can start slowly, and gradually ramp up. After a while, you will realise the benefits and transformation created by your chanting. I have been chanting Om Namah Shivaya every day for ten years now and can swear by the change it has brought about in my life.

MAGIC ON THE MOUNTAIN

As I previously mentioned, the day Chhavi and I returned to Mumbai after our trip to Babaji's Cave, both of us couldn't wait to go back. We had never felt like this about any other trip we had been on before. A year later, in November 2012, we were once again aboard the train that would take us to Kathgodam, then by bus to Nainital, Ranikhet and finally to Babaji's Cave on the Dronagiri mountain.

On this pilgrimage, there were twenty-seven of us. Like the previous trip, a day after resting at Ranikhet, we were bright and fresh the next morning, ready to travel to the mountain and start the journey that would take us to the Cave.

The first time I had trekked up the Cave, I had hurried up, trying to compete with the other pilgrims. This time, I decided to do precisely the opposite. Chhavi and I walked at a moderate pace, almost deliberately trying to be the last of the pilgrims, and took our own time to complete the trek. We decided that if we did it this way, once we reached the cave, we would be relaxed and comfortable as opposed to being exhausted and breathless like the first time. After all, we were Babaji's guests, so what was the need to hurry? If He had called us, He would be waiting for us!

When we began our trek, Daya from Ananda Sangha requested us to maintain silence and to go inwards, keeping our thoughts focused on Babaji. I decided that we would make our walking and climbing a part of our meditation exercise.

As I walked up the mountain, I began mentally conversing with Babaji. In my years of being a spiritual seeker, I have learned that when you communicate from your heart, the great masters listen. There is no better way of connecting with the higher powers than merely conversing with them as friends.

I asked Babaji, 'Babaji, how can I help you? What can I do to make your spiritual endeavours reach more people? Babaji, I am a technology guy. I work on internet and mobile projects. How can I work for you, given that my line of work is so different from yours? Babaji, how can I assist you in your mission?' These were the constant streams of thoughts that kept coursing through my mind as I climbed up the mountain.

The climb to Babaji's Cave takes about one hour amidst lush green valleys, clouds, forests and mountains. It is beautiful and gorgeously scenic. The path offers sweeping views of the beautiful Kumaon region, dotted with cosy huts with their smoking chimneys. The walk feels as if it is amidst a picturesque postcard that has actually come alive!

Forty minutes into the journey, Chhavi and I saw two men, walking towards us from the opposite side of the narrow path. As the men came closer, I realised they were holy men. One of them was dressed in a dark saffron robe, while the slightly older sage wore a white one.

When a few feet distance remained between us, Chhavi and I stopped walking and bowed down to the men, with deep respect and reverence. As a practice, we bow and do namaste to sages and holy men whenever we meet them. It is a simple act of showing respect. The two saints noticed us. The one in the saffron clothes smiled, took a few steps forward and started a light conversation with me. He enquired where we were from, whether I liked being in the mountains and the difference I felt between the city and the hills. Being a talkative person, I actively started chatting with the sage. All this time, the saint in the white robe said nothing. He stood at a fixed distance from us and looked at Chhavi and me expressionlessly.

After general inquiries, the sage in saffron looked at me intently and asked, 'Do you meditate?' I said, 'Yes Sir, I do.' The sage gazed at me and smiled. He paused for a moment. Then, slowly, as if he was delivering a special message, said, 'Just meditate. What you are supposed to do will be told to you.'

I heard him and gently nodded. At that moment, I did not pay too much attention to the words he had spoken. A brief pause later, I began talking to him about our trip to the Cave and how much we enjoyed it.

While conversing, I was on a mountain path that was quite narrow. Since the two of us were standing together, I was very close to the edge. A lady pilgrim who had been trailing us caught up with our group, saw me standing dangerously and loudly exclaimed, 'Alok, watch out! You are right at the edge of the mountain!'

As the lady's loud warning resonated around us, the sage in the saffron robes looked at her, then turned his gaze at me, gently smiled and said, 'Oh, don't worry. He will take care. Nothing will happen.' The way he said these words, he made it seem as if a higher power, unknown to us, governed the mountain and everything that happened on it.

We continued to talk, and the sage went on to tell me about how nature was being tampered with by the relentless construction activities in sacred places and the pristine mountains. He seemed disturbed by the ecological imbalance. If I had just been patient and a good listener, the sage would have spoken a lot more. But I was restless to move on and displayed my impatience. When I think about this, I realise how foolish I was. I should have just shut up and listened. Six months later, in June of 2013, Uttarakhand suffered the country's worst-ever natural disaster since the tsunami of 2004. Substantial losses occurred due to the mismanaged construction on the fragile land and the river beds of the region. It seemed as though the sage had predicted the disaster that was to come.

Our conversation over, the sage smiled and raised his palm to bless Chhavi and me. We bowed to him and then looked in the direction of the sage in white, still standing at some distance from us. Even at that moment, the sage in white did not move, nor did he acknowledge our obeisance. We all moved on.

We had another half-an-hour of climbing to complete, and I did not give our meeting and conversation with the two sages much thought. I focused on the upward trek. About forty minutes later, we reached the cave and took turns to complete our meditations inside. In the evening, we trekked down on the same route and drove back to Ranikhet. The next morning, we went to the Kathgodam station to catch the train back to Delhi.

Daya and Keshava always concluded their pilgrimages in a fun and special way. At dinner time, just before boarding our train, all of us sat together in a circle, in a cosy banquet hall in Kathgodam, and shared our own unique experiences of the pilgrimage. While there was no compulsion to share, most pilgrims contributed and revealed their individual perspective of what they were taking away from their journey.

A lady from Delhi began to speak gently. She said, 'There were two sages dressed in white and saffron, whom I met while walking up the path to the cave. The white-robed sage did not speak to me, but the one in saffron was amazing. In the few minutes that I had with him, he answered the question that had been bothering me when I had begun my trek. It seemed as if he had read my mind and told me what I needed to hear.'

As she said these words, I remembered my own experience. Just before I had started my trek, I had been pleading with Babaji and asking him how I could work for him and help him. Then, a while later, the same sage in the orange robe had told me, 'Meditate. What you need to do will be told to you.' How did he know the question I was asking Babaji? How did he provide me with an answer? The more I thought about the coincidence, the more I was convinced that my meeting with the sage was no ordinary event.

As the lady chatted about her extraordinary experience, many other pilgrims interrupted the lady excitedly. They had all had the same encounter—the sage in saffron had answered the question on their minds. When my turn came, I excitedly narrated my story, too. Many of the pilgrims had tears in their eyes as they realised the miracle that they had experienced.

Towards the end of the session, almost all the pilgrims had shared their stories. Just two ladies remained. One of them started to speak and said, 'I also met the same sages, yet barely talked to them. I was more keen to reach the Cave early and try and earn more meditation time for myself. Once I was in the Cave, I began fervently meditating on Babaji and pleading with him to give me darshan. I must have been in dhyana (meditation) for a long time. A feeling of great calm came over me and then I heard a gentle voice in my head that whispered, "I just met you today … ". The lady pilgrim was visibly emotional when she narrated her story.

As we began dinner, we chatted about these two sages and wondered who they were. We knew we had experienced something quite divine. The question on everyone's mind was: Who were these holy men?

Back in Mumbai, a week later, I was sitting on my meditation mat in my room. Just after completing my meditation, I began a mental conversation with Babaji and gently asked Him, 'Babaji, please tell me who the two sages were. What was the connection between you and them?' I received no answer. But I did not rest either. I kept pleading with Babaji to answer my question.

The very next day, I was browsing the new Facebook group Chhavi managed, called Mahavatar Babaji's Cave. We had taken a sankalpa (resolution) to create awareness about Babaji's Cave on social media, and I had created Facebook and Twitter accounts for this initiative. As I looked at the timeline of the group, I noticed that Manu Khanna—a pilgrim from our first trip to the Cave—had posted a picture on the group. Manu had not been part of the second trip. When I looked at the image she had posted, a shiver ran down my spine. This was a miniature poster painting of the great masters. In it, Babaji was wearing a light saffron dhoti, Lahiri Mahasaya was wearing a white dhoti, his guru Yukteshwar Guru was wearing saffron robes and Paramhansa Yogananda was in darker, ochre-red clothes. The clothes the masters were wearing in the picture were a perfect match for the clothes of the two sages we had met on the mountain!

It was a fantastic coincidence that Manu had posted a picture on her own, a day after I had pestered Babaji to answer a question that was puzzling me. The answer was so beautiful. We had met the great masters on the mountain, and they had blessed all of us.

Connecting the Dots

Listening attentively, without distractions, is probably one of the easiest routes to material and spiritual success. We must master the ability to listen and listen patiently. It's not easy. Our chattering mind often wants to hear what is only of our interest. It rejects messages that don't involve or engage us. The discipline one must cultivate is to listen to all words with equal attention and then decide which ones to dwell on deeper. The important lesson is to focus on the message and not on the messenger.

Exercise

Close your eyes and try and remember some of the people you may have recently met and their conversations with you. Did you pay attention to what they were saying or did you interrupt them often? Did they say something that you knew was true but did not want to accept? Were you so eager to prove your point and demonstrate your knowledge that you cut their conversations short?

Going forward, can you resolve to be patient with strangers you meet and simply listen to them? Can you try this for just one week and analyse how it helps you?

MAHARAJ-JI'S SUMPTUOUS TREAT

Neem Karoli Baba or Maharaj-ji as he was fondly called by his disciples, was the loving and magical Indian spiritual guru who gained immense popularity in the mid-Seventies. One famous fan of Maharaj-ji was Steve Jobs. Jobs wanted to seek Neem Karoli Baba's blessings but arrived in India a few months after Maharaj-ji had left his body. Many years later, Steve Jobs suggested to Mark Zuckerberg, the founder of Facebook, to visit Maharaj-ji's ashram while he was visiting India. Jobs revealed that he had experienced a profound clarity in his vision for Apple when he had visited Maharaj-ji's ashram.

The ashram is at Kainchi, an hour's drive ahead of Nainital in the beautiful state of Uttarakhand. Kainchi in the local dialect refers to the two sharp hairpin bends of the road where the ashram stands. Maharaj-ji's methods and miracles are well-known and documented in several books, such as the famous *Be Here Now* and *Miracle of Love* by Ram Dass. I would strongly recommend that you read these books. Amongst the many stories written about him, the most endearing stories I have read are about how Maharaj-ji loved to feed his disciples and prepare feasts for them.

As luck would have it, Maharaj-ji's ashram is on the route to Babaji's Cave while travelling from Kathgodam to Ranikhet, as well as on the return journey. On our Cave trips, our guides halt the buses at Kainchi and encourage the pilgrims to visit the ashram and temple premises. We spend our time at the ashram praying, meditating and indulging ourselves in eating delicious food.

The highlights of my visit to the ashram are the food dhabas (stalls) near the entrance. These tiny, ramshackle, hole-in-the-wall shops serve hot pakoras, delicious parathas, and mouth-watering tangy curries with steaming hot rice. The shikanji (lime water) made with chilled bottled and soda water along with a dash of green herbs and green chillies will keep you salivating for days. Food is my weakness, particularly North Indian food and the treats outside Maharaj-ji's ashram are irresistible.

On every visit to the ashram, which usually turns out to be a short one, my dilemma is to decide how much time I should spend meditating inside the ashram premises (the real purpose of a spiritual trip) versus enjoying the sumptuous treats outside. It's always a tough choice!

On our third trip to Babaji's Cave, we were en-route to Maharaj-ji's ashram before reaching Kathgodam to board our train. Following the routine itinerary, we would take a small break at the ashram before moving ahead. That day was Dussehra—a very auspicious day on which Lord Rama defeated the ten-headed demon king Ravana. Maharaj-ji was devoted to Rama and his eyes would well up the moment someone mentioned Rama. As Keshava read stories of

Maharaj-ji and described how he took extreme care of his devotees, a sad thought crossed my mind. I wondered, 'Why was I born so many years later that denied me the chance to meet Neem Karoli Baba? How I wish I had been one of his devotees and enjoyed his heart-warming love, affection and care.' I felt envious of the devotees that Keshava described in the stories he read aloud. Maharaj-ji never liked his devotees to be hungry. He often said, 'Feed people, serve people.'

We were nearing the ashram when Keshava completed his story. He said, 'Folks, we will be arriving at Neem Karoli Baba's ashram in a few minutes. This time, we cannot spend much time at the ashram, since we are running late. So let's do a quick darshan, and assemble back in the bus.'

When I heard Keshava's instructions, I was disappointed. It was almost 1.30 p.m in the afternoon, and I was starving. In the bus, I had been dreaming of the delicious pakoras and hot curries that were waiting for me at the dhabhas. Now, just like that, Keshava was asking me to sacrifice them! I quietly whispered to Chhavi, 'I'm starving. Let me eat first and then go inside the ashram to meditate.' Chhavi was visibly disappointed by my comment and reprimanded me. She said, 'Alok, get a grip on yourself and your addiction to your senses! We have come to Maharaj-ji's ashram and instead of going inside and meditating, you want to spend your time eating parathas?'

Chhavi's scolding made me feel guilty, so I grudgingly accepted her advice and went inside the ashram to meditate. As I sat down cross-legged in the same verandah where Maharaj-ji would often be seated, my mind went back to the hot, black gram curry usually served with snowy white rice across the road. I thought I could even smell it from where I was sitting!

Half-an-hour later, when we had completed our meditations, we began heading back towards the bus. As I glanced at the time, I sensed that there was a small window of time to indulge in my long-desired 'pet puja' (honouring the tummy). I dashed into one of the food stalls on the side and requested the owner to get me hot aloo parathas, spicy curry and all sorts of assorted pakoras. I was determined to enjoy the dhaba food I loved so much.

Some minutes later, just as the hot aloo parathas arrived at my table, a few pilgrims from our group hurriedly entered the stall. Looking directly at me, they said, 'There is a special puja (ceremony) in the ashram. The head priests have invited us to come and attend it. Please come immediately. We have to go there now.'

I was very disappointed. Grudgingly, I left my aloo parathas and golden pakoras and stomped back to the ashram. While walking, I thought to myself, 'How many meditations am I destined to do today? How will I survive with so much hunger?'

A minute later, we were inside the ashram premises. As we looked around, we could not spot the puja ceremony. I politely asked a priest, 'Sir, we've been called by the head priests for a puja. Can you please tell us where it is?'

The priest looked puzzled and asked someone else. That person smiled and pointed us in the direction of a hall overlooking the back section of the ashram. There was a flight of stairs on the side that we all climbed up swiftly. Just as we entered the large hall, a senior priest greeted us warmly. He looked in my direction and said, 'We are so happy you all have come. Welcome!'

I folded my hands with respect and asked, 'Sir, where is the puja?'

The priest flashed a big smile at me and said, 'Oh, there is no puja! Today is Dussehra, a special day in the ashram, and we have an awesome feast prepared, that includes many of Maharaj-ji's favourite dishes. We know you all would be hungry and have invited all of you to eat with us.'

As I heard these words, I lost my composure and started to cry. I looked away so that no one would notice me. It had all happened so magically. I had been remorseful about not being born when Maharaj-ji was alive to enjoy his affection. When I reached the ashram premises, I was craving for food. All this, in the omnipresent spirit of Maharaj-ji who never let a single devotee of his go hungry! In his typical style, Maharaj-ji had not just arranged a meal but a lavish feast and invited all of us to enjoy it. He wanted to feed us and make us happy and satisfied.

The dishes laid out in front of me were some of the best I have ever had. Hot curries, puris, assorted sweetmeats, halwa and vegetables continually found their way to our plates. I ate to my heart's content and satiated all my pent-up hunger. I instinctively knew I would never feel hungry again when I was at Maharaj-ji's ashram.

Connecting the Dots

Just like Maslow's hierarchy of the material world, there is a similar hierarchy that operates in the spiritual realm. I have learned that all our desires, no matter how trivial or silly, should be handed over to our gurus and gods. We should not be the judge of our wants, and instead, let our masters decide what is best for us. Once you are on the path, simple desires easily get satisfied. When your heart overflows with devotion, you melt the heart of the universe. Then everything happens. My spiritual experience has been that when our hearts are pure, the universe and the masters quickly satiate our material needs so that we can aspire for higher things. I have also learned not to hide my desires when I am in the company of enlightened people. They know anyway!

Exercise

Make a list of your needs and desires. Let that list run into as many pages as needed. Don't hold back. How can you hide your wants from your creator? Then, surrender that list (physically or mentally) to your god, guru, or whomever you believe in. Let all your wishes be exposed. This way, you will give the universe a comprehensive chance to make all those things happen that are good for you, in the order it so decides.

THE INCIDENT ON THE PLANE

As the months passed, my obsession with Babaji kept growing. I discovered that this feeling was not unique to me. Many others, including Chhavi, confirmed that they felt the same way. Once Babaji enters your consciousness, you can't stop thinking of him.

A meaningful spiritual journey is like true love. First, there is that typical madness and obsession. Then comes a sense of possession. A while later, the lingering feeling of anxiety gives way to trust and comfort. Finally, you experience peace, calm and deep companionship. Spiritual intoxication is so sweet that once you experience it, you can't get enough of it.

I was in love with Babaji and yearned to meet him. I wanted to have just a glimpse of him. I knew all the stories of Babaji from *Autobiography of a Yogi* and from other books written about him. In my mind, I would imagine different situations and places where I would meet Babaji.

My mobile games startup Games2win required me to travel frequently. One day, a strange thought popped into my head. I wanted to meet Babaji at an airport! I have no idea why I thought of such a peculiar place, but I didn't bother thinking about it too much. I prayed to Babaji, 'Babaji, the whole world converges at airports, so what better place for me to meet you than there? Just like your many appearances at the Kumbh Melas (which I had read about), maybe you can grace me with your darshan at an airport? I know you appear in many disguises and forms, so maybe that's how you can reveal yourself to me? Give me one glimpse of yourself, please, Babaji.'

Just after our first trip to the Cave, I came to know that the famous south Indian actor Rajinikanth was a big fan of Babaji and has pictures of him in his house. He visits the Cave each year. What is most intriguing about Rajinikanth's connection with Babaji is a movie he made a few years ago called *Baba*. While I have not seen the complete movie (it is in Tamil), there is a famous clip of the movie on YouTube. In it, Rajinikanth goes on an amazing adventure and enjoys a fantastical journey to meet Babaji. While the movie failed commercially, by making this offbeat film, Rajinikanth revealed to the world that he was a chosen devotee of Babaji and had experienced being with Babaji. Like Rajinikanth, I, too, wanted that opportunity of meeting Babaji and to enjoy the sense of adventure that came with it.

On one business trip, I was flying from Mumbai to Delhi and returning home the same day. Just when I reached Mumbai airport, an intense 'sankalpa' (strong desire) to meet Babaji manifested in my mind. At the airport—while checking-in, walking to the departure gate, and even when I was waiting to board the aircraft—I meditated on Babaji.

Occasionally, I looked around to try and see if I could spot him! No matter how hard I looked, Babaji wasn't there. Although I felt disappointed, I kept my spirits high and prayed to him with even more conviction. As the flight took off, I consoled myself thinking that Babaji would surely meet me on the return trip to Mumbai. In my heart, I knew that Babaji would not disappoint me.

After my work was over, I reached Delhi airport in the late afternoon for my evening flight to Mumbai. Once I was inside the terminal, I once again began to meditate on Babaji and kept looking for him. Was he the balding man with the newspaper? Was he watching me from the sides where I could not spot him? When I was tired of looking everywhere, I remembered the passage in *Autobiography of a Yogi* when even the great master and saint Sri Yukteswar Giri failed to see Babaji. In one incident, when Sri Yukteswar Giri entered the room of his guru, Lahiri Mahasaya, Babaji is present, but Yukteswarji does not see him. Later, Babaji tells him, 'Child, you must meditate more. Your gaze is not yet faultless—you could not see me hiding behind the sunlight.' When I could not find Babaji, I asked myself: Was my gaze also not yet ready to spot the great Babaji?

On board the Delhi-Mumbai flight, I was seated in an aisle seat in the front section of the aircraft. I had figured that aisles were the best seats in a plane. They allowed me to extensively network (I could speak to the passengers seated next to me and those on my other side) and also provided me with the comfort of being able to move around freely. As the flight took off, my mind remained transfixed on Babaji, and I continued praying fervently for darshan.

An hour-and-a-half into the flight, the captain announced that we were approaching Mumbai and asked the cabin crew to prepare for landing. The lights of the plane dimmed gently. While fastening my seatbelt, I noticed a passenger sitting diagonally across me, holding his iPad in an odd, angular way, making it protrude from the edge of his seat. He was reading a book on his kindle and seemed to be in a hurry, flipping the pages swiftly. Suddenly, like a thunderbolt, I saw the man looking at the picture of Babaji! Instantly, I realised that the man was reading the kindle version of *Autobiography of a Yogi* that had a full-sized poster of Babaji inside it. As I stared transfixed at Babaji, the man flipped the page. And before I could think, the man did the unthinkable. He flipped back to the previous page and stared at Babaji's picture. The plane was pitch dark, and the black and white photo of Babaji shone like a star, radiating a glow around it. The man held up the page for a while. I had goosebumps all over as I realised what had just happened. Babaji had granted me darshan. I had yearned for Babaji through the day, and lo and behold, he had appeared in front of me.

My throat was dry, and I felt like crying, but no tears came. I was overwhelmed by the grace and blessings I had experienced. Only Babaji could have done what He had done. Just like the case with Parking Frenzy, this was quintessential Babaji—he would do everything to fulfil the wishes of his followers and make them happy.

After the plane landed and we got off, I hurried to find the man with the iPad. Thankfully, I saw him on the shuttle bus that was taking us to the arrivals terminal.

Without any hesitation, I went up to him and introduced myself. Interestingly, he had heard of my work as a digital entrepreneur and introduced himself. He was Kaushika Madhavan who worked at A.T. Kearney. (Kaushika is now the managing partner and country head of Kearney India.)

Without wasting any time, I said, 'Sir, just around the time we were landing, you were reading *Autobiography of a Yogi* on your kindle. As you flipped the pages, you came across Babaji's picture. Later, you again flipped back to look at the picture. What made you do that?'

Kaushika seemed a bit puzzled and replied, 'I'm not so sure! Honestly, I haven't even read the book completely. I just opened it in the aircraft and flipped through the pages. I am not even sure who Babaji is!'

I was amazed to realise that Kaushika was neither a Babaji fan nor an avid reader of *Autobiography of a Yogi*. Just at that time, he had randomly opened that book and turned to the specific page that had Babaji's picture in it. His actions were not mere coincidence. They were the act of extraordinary grace.

When I thought about this incident, even more, I realised that the vast majority of the kindle versions of *Autobiography of a Yogi* downloaded were the free versions, which did not have Babaji's picture (that edition has no images). Amazingly, Kaushika had bought the paid version of the e-book and had been the instrument to give me Babaji's darshan, in an aircraft, nonetheless.

Connecting the Dots

The Bhagavad Gita mentions three paths to salvation. They are Jnana Yoga (path of knowledge), Karma Yoga (path of action) and Bhakti Yoga (path of devotion). In my experience, Bhakti Yoga is the simplest. When one has complete and utmost devotion towards his master and prays and pleads to him with the innocence of a child, the guru gives in. While I have only narrated a few incidents in this book of the demands I made of Babaji, I have hounded him many more times for silly favours. Each time, he has granted me my wishes. Only after multiple gifts did I realise how juvenile and shallow my behaviour was. The great gurus pamper their devotees to let them bloom in their spiritual journey, just like caring parents indulge their small children who later flourish into responsible adults.

Exercise

Gently close your eyes and reflect on the times you have asked for small gifts and favours with complete devotion and fervent prayers. Haven't you received what you wanted? If you haven't, try it! Ask for what your heart desires and utterly devote yourself to the higher power you believe in to help you fulfil it. I can assure you of guaranteed success.

AIRPORT GATES

Airports and I have a karmic connection. After my miracle with Babaji, I continued to experience magical moments at airports, particularly at airport gates.

Frankfurt Airport

I had practised the Sudarshan Kriya for many years. The benefits of the kriya were immense. My occasional fondness for alcohol and cigarettes had dropped away. I gained heightened abilities of intuition, forbearance and creativity. My life had beautifully fallen into place, and when my heart yearned for something, it would easily manifest.

One day at Mumbai airport, just as I had passed through the security check, I felt a strong intuition that my guru Sri Sri was sitting near an airport gate, surrounded by his followers. The feeling was so strong that I was sure Guruji was at the airport. I slowly walked up to my gate that was at the far end of the terminal, and I looked everywhere for him but realised that Guruji wasn't there. I never understood why I had this experience. Over the next few years, I would experience the same feeling, repeatedly. Yet, I never met

Sri Sri even once. I continued to travel, conduct my meetings, meet exciting people, and come back home, weary, tired, yet fulfilled.

As my mobile gaming startup started to scale, I began travelling to California frequently. My investors were based there, and I had set up a small office in San Francisco. On one such trip, after completing my work in the US, I was flying back from San Francisco to Mumbai via Frankfurt. At that time, I was aware that Guruji had embarked on his regular European tour and would be visiting the Art of Living Ashram in Germany. When I landed in Frankfurt, I wondered if Sri Sri was still in Germany at that time. To find out, I messaged Sri Sri's international secretary and requested information about his whereabouts. In a few minutes, I received a message informing me that Guruji was in Frankfurt that day but was heading back to Delhi in a few hours. The secretary advised me that Guruji was just about to leave for the airport, and there was no opportunity to meet him in the city.

When I read this update, my head began to buzz! I was at Frankfurt airport, too. Given my frequent travels, I knew flight schedules well and remembered that the Frankfurt-Mumbai and Frankfurt-Delhi flights departed almost at the same time from Frankfurt airport. If Guruji was coming to the airport to fly to Delhi, surely his flight time would be similar to mine. Quickly, I checked the departure screens and was stunned to read that not only were the two flights leaving at the same time, but their departure gates were next to each other.

My heart began to beat faster. I remembered my recurring vision of meeting Sri Sri at an airport gate, surrounded by his followers. Was this the day for my dream to materialise?

As I waited, time passed by slowly. I kept looking at the end of the hall to spot the familiar entourage of Art of Living devotees. In trademark style, they would arrive half-walking, half-running, carrying flowers, shawls and presents, with my guru Sri Sri walking regally, in their midst.

I heard the boarding announcement of my Mumbai flight, and the one for the Delhi flight a few minutes later. I felt uneasy. Even though it was time for all of us to board, no one from Art of Living had turned up yet. I kept my cool and hung around at the gate of the Delhi flight. As the minutes ticked past, the vast swathe of passengers boarding the Mumbai flight began to get thinner and thinner until there were just a few people left. A couple of minutes later, I heard the last and final boarding call for my flight. Yet, I was determined to meet Guruji and kept waiting in the sitting area, facing the departure gate of the Delhi flight.

A few more precious minutes passed. I noticed there were no more passengers in the queue for the Mumbai flight. That meant that everyone had boarded the flight. Just when I was about to rush towards the gate, I spotted Rajita Kulkarni, a veteran of the Art of Living and one of Sri Sri's most trusted confidants. She was walking briskly towards the gate of the Mumbai flight. Instinctively, I knew that if Rajita had arrived, Sri Sri would appear soon, since Rajita often travelled with Gurujii. I excitedly ran up to her and asked, 'Hi Rajita-ji, where is Guruji?'

Rajita was surprised to see me at the gate, and said, 'Oh, Alok, how are you? It's nice to see you here! I am sure you wanted to meet Guruji, but he is already on the plane! Guruji normally boards planes via VIP security protocols which operate through special gates. Guruji is now already on his seat!'

My face lost its colour, and my disappointment was evident. I sighed loudly. Sensing my grief, Rajita said, 'Alok, at least let me make you talk to Guruji. I am sure he will like to speak to you.' As I composed myself, Rajita dialled Sri Sri on her mobile phone and gave me the handset.

As I gingerly placed the phone near my ear, I heard my guru's sweet voice 'Haan, Alok, how are you?'

I said, 'Guruji, I am very well, but very disappointed that I could not meet you just now. I was waiting and waiting for you at the gate.'

Guruji paused for a while and said, 'I know, Alok, but what can I do? These people brought me in from a different entrance. Anyway, we will meet soon, okay?'

I said, 'Yes, Guruji, we will. Jai Gurudev.'

I bade farewell to Rajita, rushed towards my departure gate and just about caught my flight. As I sat down on my seat, I felt crushed from the inside. I had missed my golden opportunity to meet Guruji. 'How could such a coincidence ever take place again?' I thought to myself.

Dubai Airport

Two years after the Frankfurt airport incident, I received a call from the Art of Living headquarters in Bangalore.

Sri Sri's secretary Jaina Desai was on the line. Jaina came straight to the point and asked me, 'Alok, Guruji wants to know if you are free in the next few weeks.'

I instantly understood that this was one of those rare moments in a devotee's life when the Master chooses him for an important task. I said, 'Of course, Jaina, I am free.' (Coincidentally, there was no travel planned for me in those weeks, nor did I have any critical meetings scheduled.)

As anticipated, Guruji had chosen me for an important assignment. Three weeks later, I was one of a four-member team that Sri Sri had handpicked to travel with him to Iraq. The President of the Kurdistan Region, Nechirvan Barzani, had invited Guruji to come to Iraq and spend some time touring his country. The President wanted Sri Sri to assess the peace-keeping missions in Kurdistan and also bless the refugees. Our invitation was to travel to Erbil—the capital of the Kurdistan Region in Northern Iraq—as official guests of President Barzani.

The itinerary for the group was to travel from Bangalore to Dubai, stay overnight at the Airport Hotel, and then board an early morning flight to Erbil the next day.

It was so exciting for me to travel with Guruji! Everyone at the Bangalore airport not only knew him but seemed to be his devotees as well. Walking past immigration and security checks at the airport felt so different when Guruji was a co-passenger.

We flew to Dubai and checked into the Airport Hotel for a short rest. At 4 a.m. the next day, we woke up and began getting ready for the long day ahead. An hour later, we were ready and waited for Guruji in the lobby of the hotel. I distinctively remember staring at the Omega watches on the hotel's reception wall displaying the time of the famous cities in the world. Almost forty minutes passed by. We anxiously kept looking towards Guruji's room and hoped it would open soon. As per the departure screen, the flight to Erbil was on schedule, and we needed to get going. As we waited, two hostesses from the Dubai airport service, Marhaba, arrived to escort us to our departure gate. The ladies were puzzled to see us sitting in the lobby. We explained to them that we were expecting our 'boss' to emerge soon from the room. They looked surprised and reiterated that we needed to head towards the departure gates since it was a long walk away. We were all a bit tense and waited anxiously for Guruji.

A few minutes later, Sri Sri emerged from his room, looking supremely radiant. He flashed his trademark smile that made all our worries disappear. Guruji was wearing his classic white attire, beautifully adorned with a coloured decorative border, and matched with a gorgeous shawl. The moment Guruji noticed us, he warmly enquired about how we slept and if we were feeling refreshed. We became engrossed chatting with him until one of the Marhaba ladies caught my attention and made gestures to start walking towards our Erbil flight.

I looked at Sri Sri and gently said, 'Guruji, shall we go? We will be late otherwise'. Guruji looked at me, smiled and said, 'Haan … Alok, we will leave, but what is the hurry?' He resumed talking to the other devotees and instructed them to follow up on some of the daily chores of the ashram.

We had no choice but to wait. About ten long minutes later, anxiety got the better of me. I looked beseechingly at Guruji and said, 'Guruji, please let's go. We have a flight to catch, and it seems we may already be a bit late.' Just as I finished speaking, Sri Sri gave me the most beautiful smile I've ever seen. I still remember it as if it happened a few moments ago. And that was it. Sri Sri stayed where he was, as did all of us devotees!

Observing the placid devotees and the calm, composed 'Boss' (Guruji), the Marhaba ladies went into complete panic mode. They mumbled to each other until one of them told me, 'Sir, why doesn't your boss start walking? Does he want to miss his flight? Why can't you convince him to follow us immediately? I hope you all know that the gate for the Erbil flight is very far from here?'

In this unfolding airport drama, I felt caught between a rock and a hard place. As a seasoned traveller, I always preferred to arrive at departure gates ahead of time to avoid last-minute panic and confusion. But in this particular case, Guruji seemed to be in no hurry! I knew what a stickler Guruji was for adhering to schedules, yet this morning, he was playing truant with all of us!

Another ten more minutes passed. I was in a state of panic. I went up to Sri Sri and firmly said, 'Guruji, please let's go now? I seriously think we should not delay any more.'

Sri Sri looked at me and smiled. For a few microseconds, I saw the depth of a million galaxies in his eyes. Time just froze as I looked at him. Then, he shrugged his shoulders and gestured that he was ready to move ahead, albeit very reluctantly. Taking my cue, our entire group started walking towards the departure gate, with the Marhaba ladies leading the way.

A good fifteen minutes later, we arrived at the departure gate for the Erbil flight. Almost immediately, I sensed that something was not right. There were too many people milling around the departure area, and the place was hot and stuffy. I hurried to the departure gate of the flight and asked the airline staff about the current status. (I was panicking that the plane had left.) The airline staff seemed busy multi-tasking and after keeping me waiting for a while, curtly told me, 'Sorry, Sir, but the plane is not ready yet. You will have to wait for a while.' I was shocked and pointed to the departure schedules that read that the flight was to leave on time. They just shrugged their shoulders and asked me to be patient for their announcement.

Distraught by the uncertainty and delay of the flight, I started looking around for clean, empty seats to make Guruji comfortable. Unfortunately, for some strange reason, the entire departure hall was packed to the brim. There was not a single place available to sit. To makes things worse, the air-conditioning was not functioning. We were in a complete mess.

Despite the dismal conditions, I did not lose hope. I went up to a few young passengers and humbly requested them to vacate their seats for Guruji, but they flatly refused. I was shocked. I had never come across such insensitive people before.

When all my efforts had failed, I walked back to Guruji, feeling defeated and tired. I looked at him and said, 'Guruji, this is a hopeless situation. The flight has still not arrived, the air-conditioning does not work, and there is not a single seat available for you to sit on! I'm very sorry for having brought you here.'

Sri Sri looked at me with extreme tenderness and gently laughed. Then he softly said, 'But Alok, I told you there was no hurry to come here in the first place!' The moment Guruji spoke these words, I knew he had known (how, I don't know!) all along that our flight was late and that the departure terminal was a mess. He had tried his best to stay back at the hotel, but I had insisted that all of us hurry up. That day I learned an important lesson in my life—never question your guru and simply listen to his instructions. He always knows better than you do.

Abu Dhabi Airport

I kept my peace-keeping trip to Iraq a well-guarded secret. For years, Iraq had topped the list of the most dangerous places in the world. When I decided to travel there with Guruji, I did not feel the need to share the information with even my parents or my children. I did not want them to be unduly worried. In my heart, I knew that I was travelling with my guru, and he would take care of me. I only told Chhavi and a couple of close associates. While planning the paperwork for the Iraqi visa, I received feedback that Iraqi stamps were frowned upon at global airports and especially in the US. Most immigration officers would be alarmed about my intentions of travelling to such a dangerous country. If I was a mobile gaming entrepreneur and had an extensive business in the US, what was I doing in Iraq? What sort of gaming business happened there? Even if I mentioned 'peace-keeping' as my purpose, who would believe me? Was peace-keeping something that I regularly did? What would happen if I would be refused entry to the US? Had my VCs funded me to focus on peace-keeping and travelling to Iraq? These thoughts stressed me considerably and made me feel bogged down.

While my negative thoughts became too much, I sat down and meditated on them. I surrendered my doubts and problems to my guru. A while later, a peaceful feeling came over me. I instinctively understood that if my guru had invited me to join him in his work, then he would take care of everything, including my security and my passport problems.

Our trip to Iraq was extremely successful. President Barzani was the perfect host and made sure that Sri Sri and his entourage were well taken care of, and protected. We travelled all over the Kurdistan region in black bulletproof SUVs that were supplied by the president's security team. In the four days we spent in Kurdistan, Sri Sri visited the parliament, met leaders of different religious and ethnic communities and extensively toured the UN refugee camps. Art of Living has an active presence in Iraq and has conducted significant relief operations there. Its focus has been to help the Yazidi communities who have been persecuted by extremist groups in Iraq. For me, the highlight of my trip was accompanying Sri Sri to President Barzani's house, which was was rumoured to be one of Saddam

Hussein's personal palaces. As you can imagine, it was extravagantly decorated and drop-dead gorgeous. Till that day, I had never imagined visiting the official residence of the president of a country. But then, with a guru, everything becomes possible.

The most uplifting outcome of the trip was the quality time I got to spend with my Master. What more could a devotee ask for than to be in the presence of his guru for days on end? I would sit in the evening at the feet of Guruji while he conducted his affairs. Often, he would be flipping TV channels or taking phone calls from all over the world. Just before dinner, I would compose some of Guruji's tweets, summarising the events of the day. My four days in Iraq are etched in my mind as some of the most memorable days of my life.

On our trip back to India, we were to fly from Erbil to Abu Dhabi and then take connecting flights to our respective destinations. At Erbil airport, we were given a full State send-off, with red carpets, oversized bouquets and military salutes. Once I was comfortably seated in the aircraft, one of the devotees handed me my passport. (We had surrendered our passports to him on arrival, and he was responsible for their safe-keeping.) The moment I got mine back, I hurriedly began to flip the pages to check all the places where the Iraqi immigration stamps appeared and how prominently they stood out. As I scanned my passport, I did not notice any stamp marks. I was sure I had not looked carefully enough, so I did a re-scan, taking my time to go through all my passport pages, one by one. I was amazed when I reached the end and did not find any Iraqi stamp inside! I couldn't believe it. Was this because we were invitees of the president and not subject to usual passport control? Whatever the reason was, I was very relieved! My fears of having objectionable markings on my passport instantly disappeared. On a higher level, this was a simple demonstration of how a guru operated. He understood his devotees' needs and silently took care of them. All I needed to do was to surrender and have faith!

A few hours later, we landed at Abu Dhabi and proceeded to pass through immigration. We accompanied Sri Sri to the business lounge and took turns chatting with him. About an hour later, we began walking to our departure gate. I was walking side by side with Guruji.

Just as we entered the main departure gate area, people noticed Guruji and began to rush towards him. In just a few minutes, a crowd had gathered, and they kept asking Sri Sri for blessings, selfies and pats on their heads. It seemed as if everyone at the airport knew him.

After Guruji had dispensed with one large gathering, he gently told me, 'Alok, come, let us sit down a few seats ahead, with our backs to the crowds. This way, the crowds will not notice me, and we will enjoy some peace. Later, we will walk to our departure gate.' I was delighted by the idea and found an isolated area near an inactive airport gate for us to sit down. Guruji asked the accompanying Art of Living devotees to go and shop for themselves and their families.

I realised that I was all alone with Guruji. For the next twenty minutes, I sat beside him without any distractions.

I spoke little and just focused on being in his presence that felt powerfully magnetic and uplifting. At one point, he even interlocked his arm into mine, as best of friends do. We said nothing and just revelled in each other's company.

A while later, I noticed the inactive departure gate on my left side. Instantly, my mind connected with the persistent desire I had harboured for many years of meeting Guruji at an airport gate. I was doing just that, sitting quietly with him. It was such a fantastic moment. Guruji had not only fulfilled that simple wish of mine but also given me an experience that I would cherish for my lifetime.

Connecting the Dots

One of the most effective ways to achieve success is by having infinite patience, while making a solid relentless effort. 'Titiksha' (forbearance) is a spiritual principle that asks you to wait to realise your dream. In our lives today, we have been spoilt by instant gratification. The habit of expecting efforts to bear fruit almost immediately makes us forget the power of infinite patience naturally bestowed on us. In the spiritual realm, instant gifts are rare. But blessings and rewards by having patience are guaranteed. In my case, I waited and waited for years until my dream came true, without any special effort on my part. All I did was to have patience.

Exercise

Close your eyes and promise to build your ability to practise patience and forbearance. Know that what you want will come to you, but it will take its own time. Don't be impatient while expecting the fruit of your actions. Think of something that you promise to be patient about, and surrender your pledge to the universe.

I DON'T KNOW HOW PRAWNS TASTE

By 2015, Chhavi and I had firmly established ourselves in spiritual practices. I found a magical balance in my work as a digital startup entrepreneur and as a committed spiritual practitioner and teacher. Neither of us felt the need to attend events, parties and social gatherings, and engage ourselves in frivolous banter. Life was beautiful and without any distractions!

A new habit we did cultivate was of spiritual tourism—visiting spiritual places that had become famous for devotees.

One such place we fell in love with was Pondicherry. Beyond its quaint streets with French names and the city's charming vibe, our top attraction of the city was the ashram of Sri Aurobindo and the Mother. We could spend hours sitting near their samadhis, absorbing the incredible peace that permeated the entire courtyard. Meditating at that place was effortless. We occasionally also meditated at the Matri Mandir at Auroville, a few kilometres away from the city.

As our trips to Pondicherry became more frequent, a close friend of ours introduced us to Vijay Poddar, a distinguished and soft-spoken trustee of the Sri Aurobindo

Ashram. Each time we arrived in Pondicherry, we would meet Vijay Bhai in the spacious parlour of his large colonial bungalow, in the centre of the city. We would chat, discuss our spiritual progress and seek special evening passes that would give us entry to the ashram premises during non-visiting hours.

A meaningful spiritual journey is never complete without tough challenges. As much as a devotee trains himself to be humble and grounded, his mind is seldom in his control. It can often trick, confuse and exaggerate things. It can tempt us to make mistakes and behave in ways we never imagined. On one particular trip to Pondicherry, I became a victim of the machinations of my mind.

It was mid-October 2016, and Chhavi and I were comfortably seated in Vijay Bhai's grand home. We had arrived in Pondicherry that afternoon and met him soon afterwards to say hello and secure our evening passes. After the simple pleasantries were over, Vijay Bhai asked me, 'So, Alok, how are you? How has the year been? Tell me about your spiritual journey, and how you are progressing on the path.'

I cannot remember what was my frame of mind that day. But when I heard his question, I replied with an unusual dose of arrogance and hubris. I said, 'Vijay Bhai, I am doing well! Spirituality is working well for me. As you know, I do not eat non-vegetarian food. Now, thanks to my kriya practices, I have also dropped alcohol completely!'

He gently smiled and ignoring my vain proclamations, merely said, 'Oh, Alok, that is so nice to hear. Yes, once you are on the path, all our negative addictions start to fade away...'

I did not let Vijay Bhai complete what he wanted to say and interrupted him by saying, 'Sir, honestly, what has happened to me is magical. The memory of alcohol has left my mind. It's as if I don't ever remember drinking at all!'

He smiled and looked at me earnestly, hoping that I would not continue boasting about my spiritual gains. He said, 'Keep meditating. Make sure you maintain your discipline. Staying in practice is the secret, right?'

When a person's mind is feverish, it is not in his control. Such was my case. I went on and said, 'Vijay Bhai, actually you have not understood my point at all. Let me explain this again to you. It's a bit like how I've been born a vegetarian and thus never had the chance of eating non-vegetarian food. So, if someone asks me if I like the taste of prawns, I will not be able to answer, because I have never eaten prawns. I have no memory of eating them. My explanation for alcohol is the same. Suddenly, I don't remember the taste or pleasure of drinks, because the memory of alcohol has vanished from my mind!'

As I delivered my boast with great aplomb, I saw Vijay Bhai smiling at me, but with grave concern on his face. Clearly, he was troubled about my boasting, as I realised later.

We chatted a bit more, collected our evening passes, and left Vijay Bhai's house to head to the ashram. After an hour of blissful meditation, we headed back to our hotel. While we were walking, Chhavi suddenly asked me, 'Alok, why did you tell Vijay Bhai that you don't know the taste of prawns? I mean, from where did prawns come into your mind? Usually, someone would give a similar example by saying chicken or some other popular food, but you said prawns. I wonder from where you got that idea?'

I laughed and haughtily told Chhavi, 'It is an extreme example to prove how distant I am from non-vegetarian food. In life, sometimes, even vegetarians accidentally taste chicken, but they never taste prawns. So, I said prawns!'

Chhavi was puzzled by my answer but did not press me further. I knew she was unhappy about my boasting of my spiritual progress. The evening was crisp and fresh, and we continued our walk back to Le Dupleix—our favourite hotel in Pondicherry. Designed by French architects, this boutique hotel exudes a beautiful colonial charm and is very small and private. We had booked our favourite room in the hotel and enjoyed the simple luxuries it offered.

By the time we reached the hotel, I was starving. We quickly refreshed ourselves in the room and headed downstairs for dinner. Le Dupleix has a simple restaurant that serves all meals. Given our frequent visits, the staff knew us well. After being seated, the manager came across to our table to take our order. As a habit, I like to have a hot soup before dinner, and since we were in Pondicherry, the soul of South India, I planned to treat myself to a hot rasam, a South Indian delicacy. It's a watery tomato soup which is quite spicy. A tasty rasam can invigorate the palate and activate latent hunger.

I asked the manager, 'Boss, do you have a good rasam soup?'

He immediately nodded and said, 'Sir, the best in Pondicherry!'

Noting his confidence, I instantly ordered a rasam for myself. Chhavi passed on it since she avoids spicy food. We also ordered palak paneer, mixed vegetable raita and tandoori rotis for our main course.

Fifteen minutes later, a waiter arrived and served me the rasam. It was steaming hot, and the aroma made my mouth water. Almost immediately, I sank my soup spoon in it and carefully sipped it. It tasted a bit different and wasn't quite the rasam flavour I was used to eating, but I wasn't giving up on my favourite soup so fast. I took a few more sips and noticed some chunky nuggets mixed in it. I took a large spoon of rasam and the chunks at the bottom and savoured them in my mouth.

Instantly, I knew something was wrong. This soup didn't taste like a typical, tangy rasam. It had an unpleasant smell, and the nuggets were white and chewy.

I called the manager and told him, 'I'm sorry, but this rasam isn't tasty! It's got a peculiar smell. Are you sure this is the recipe of the regular South Indian rasam available everywhere?' The manager's face fell when he heard my question. He looked concerned and softly said, 'Sir, this is special prawn rasam soup. It is the speciality of our hotel and quite famous in Pondicherry. There are prawns in the soup, not vegetables.'

When the manager mentioned prawns, my mind went numb. I closed my eyes for a few seconds, and when I opened them, I noticed Chhavi looking at me. At that very moment,

I realised the lesson I had just learned. All evening, I had boasted about not knowing what prawns tasted like and had eaten spoonfuls of them just now. I now knew exactly how prawns tasted.

The embarrassed manager understood the faux pas and began to apologise frantically. I looked at him, folded my hands, did a namaste and decided not to make an issue of this incident. Little did he know of the role he had played in my spiritual journey and upliftment. I looked at the rasam and the prawns inside, one last time, did a namaste to them and then closed my eyes. I remembered Mother and Sri Aurobindo and thanked them for this magical experience and lesson. With one simple stroke, they had taught me never to be arrogant.

Connecting the Dots

Arrogance or 'ghamand' (the Hindi word for pride) is a natural human emotion. While it may survive (for a while) unchecked in the material world, there is no place for vanity in the devotee who aspires to achieve spiritual success. Talking about your spiritual progress is frowned upon and should be avoided at any cost. Neem Karoli Baba 'Maharaj-ji' famously said, 'You should not talk about your wealth, wife, or sadhana, or they will go away.'

Luckily for me, I only had my silly pride taken away by a harmless life-changing lesson in Pondicherry. A guru plays this part very well. He will course-correct his disciples from colossal losses by making them endure small, short-lived pains.

Exercise

Close your eyes and take a deep breath. Exhale and relax. Can you become aware of what makes you vain or arrogant? What do you keep boasting about, whenever you get a chance? Try and focus on that aspect for a few minutes. Then, make a simple resolution to tone down your pride and make a fervent prayer to keep you grounded and humble. Resolve to dissolve your ghamand.

BABAJI IS ALWAYS AROUND

Chhavi and I have been visiting Babaji's Cave since 2011, and there have been many occasions that have assured me of Babaji's omnipresence, omnipotence and infinite grace in my life. It is beyond doubt that Babaji is always around. In *Autobiography of a Yogi*, Babaji utters these immortal words to Lahiri Mahasaya: 'I will always come when you need me.' The events that follow are my humble testimony of Babaji's sacred promise to always be there for his devotees.

Kokilaben Hospital, Mumbai

A few months after our first trip to the Cave, my older daughter needed a minor surgical procedure on her palm. To decide on the surgeon, Chhavi and I met a number of doctors and were most impressed by Dr Vimal Someshwar, who operated from Kokilaben Hospital at Versova. Even though the hospital was far away from our home, Dr Someshwar was our choice, and we admitted Anushka to that hospital.

On the day of the surgery, at 10 a.m., the nurses wheeled Anushka into the operating theatre. Chhavi and I sat on the chairs in the waiting room, a few metres away. The moment I was seated, I closed my eyes and began silently chanting 'Om Kriya Babaji, Namah Om.' It seemed like a reflex action. Within minutes, I slipped into a deep meditation. All through my meditation, I remembered Babaji and pleaded with him to be with Anushka, and make sure that everything went well.

I lost sense of time. When I opened my eyes, Chhavi was sitting next to me, quietly meditating. I then noticed an unknown number calling me on my phone. When I answered this call, I heard an unfamiliar voice.

The lady asked, 'Hi, is that Alok?'

I confirmed it was.

The lady continued, 'Do you remember me?'

I replied, 'Unfortunately, I cannot place you. I'm sorry.'

The woman chuckled a bit and said, 'Alok, I can understand. My name is Suman, and I was one of the pilgrims who had travelled to Babaji's Cave with you. Do you remember me now?' Once she had reminded me, I instantly recognised her. I politely mentioned that I was not in a position to speak to her since I was out, and promised to call her later.

Suman said, 'Of course, I understand, Alok. Honestly, I would never have called you randomly. But this morning, something strange happened. I am at home, busy with some design work going on here. I have a carpenter literally sitting on my head, constantly asking me questions. Amidst all the mayhem, I was overcome with a sudden desire to call you! I was baffled. I thought of completing my work and calling you later, but something compelled me to call you just now. I felt as if I was directed to call you. Do you think it could have been Babaji who made me feel like this?'

When I heard these words, my throat choked. I shuddered and felt goosebumps all over my body. Just a few minutes ago, I was fervently praying to Babaji to help Anushka with her surgery. Then, all of a sudden, an unknown lady called me randomly because she felt compelled by a higher power, and mentioned Babaji. Instinctively, I knew this was Babaji who had inspired Suman to pick up the phone and tell me, 'I am here and will take care of everything.'

I thanked Suman for her call and promised to call her soon. I also hinted that her hunch was right. Babaji was involved in this plot! Quickly, I returned to my seat and sat next to Chhavi in the waiting room.

After a few minutes, Dr Someshwar entered the waiting room, beaming a big smile. He looked at Chhavi and me and said, 'The procedure is over, without any issues. Anuskha is doing very well!'

I had tears in my eyes as I profusely thanked the doctor. When I looked at Chhavi, I wanted to burst out and tell her about the call from Suman. Babaji had messaged me that Anushka was doing perfectly fine, even before the doctor had come out and met us!

Breach Candy Hospital, Mumbai

A few years ago, Chhavi fell ill. She would sometimes get dizzy spells that made her weak and drained. We consulted most of the doctors we knew, but none of them could diagnose anything specific. It was a frustrating and worrisome time for both of us.

One of the specialists suggested that we get a brain MRI done just to rule out all possibilities that could be making her sick. I immediately agreed, even though Chhavi remained sceptical about going through such an elaborate test.

On my insistence, I took an appointment for an MRI test at the Breach Candy hospital in South Mumbai and reached there with Chhavi. This is one of the best hospitals I have come across in India. It serves as our default hospital for all our needs—God forbid if we have any.

From the moment we entered the MRI department, I sensed that Chhavi was uncomfortable. To stop her from walking out, I assured her that the technicians would do their job swiftly, and we would be out of the place quickly. At the back of my mind, I knew from personal experience that a complete MRI would last for at least forty minutes, and could be a very claustrophobic experience for almost anyone. Given Chhavi's dizzy spells, I had a bad feeling that this MRI would not be a smooth experience for her. To make Chhavi feel comfortable, I assured her that I would be sitting right outside the MRI machine in case she needed me.

Ten minutes later, two technicians gently laid Chhavi into the MRI stretcher and got her ready to place her in the machine. One of the technicians gave Chhavi a bell and gently told her, 'Madam, if you become uncomfortable, please ring the bell. We will immediately stop the machine and get you out.'

I clasped Chhavi's hand tightly and watched her slide into the machine's chamber. Then, I quietly sat on the nearby chair, waiting for the process to start. Barely a minute had passed when I heard Chhavi ring the alarm bell. In a few seconds, the two technicians came running in and gently extracted Chhavi from the machine. I asked her what the problem was. Chhavi said, 'I am thirsty.' The technicians gave her some water and gently slid her back into the machine.

I was hoping that Chhavi would bear the nightmarish experience and let the MRI process run its course. But five minutes later, Chhavi rang the bell again. When we got her out, she bluntly told me, 'Alok, I don't want to do this. Let's get out of here. I am fine and don't need this at all.' I begged her to bear with the discomfort so that we could complete the test once and for all. Chhavi very reluctantly agreed and went back into the machine, but just a few minutes later, rang the bell, once again.

This time, a senior technician came up to me and said, 'Sir, we cannot keep wasting time like this. Your wife is uncomfortable in the machine, so we suggest you arrange to admit her to the hospital so that we can anaesthetise her and then conduct the MRI. This method is a normal procedure for patients who are unable to tolerate the MRI process. Just now, we have many patients waiting outside, and your wife's case is becoming an impossible situation.'

I looked at the technician helplessly. In my heart, I couldn't imagine admitting Chhavi into the hospital and getting her anaesthetised for a mere MRI. I begged the technician for one more chance. He was reluctant to continue but gave in to my repeated requests. Immediately, I went back to Chhavi and told her what the technician had just told me. I hoped that the dread of anaesthesia and getting admitted to the hospital would coerce her to get the MRI completed this time.

Chhavi agreed to try again. As the technicians placed her into the machine, I remembered Babaji with all sincerity I could muster. I begged Him to help Chhavi and give her the strength to be able to go through the procedure.

A few minutes passed. The MRI machine was making loud, hammering sounds. I grew anxious and prayed to Babaji as hard as I could for the test to conclude rapidly. Just then, Chhavi rang the bell.

As we got her out, Chhavi looked very sternly at me and said, 'Alok, I can't do this anymore. Let's go.'

I agreed and helped her to her feet. As we walked out of the MRI chamber, I asked her to wait for me in the sitting area so that I could pay the bill and discuss the next steps with the technicians.

When I went up to the cashier and asked him to generate the invoice, the man said, 'Sir, since the test is incomplete, there is no need to pay just now. You can make another appointment and then pay the fees after the tests get completed.'

I thanked him for his help and began walking back to Chhavi. Just then, the senior technician whom I had met a few minutes ago came up to me and said, 'Sir, I wanted to tell you that your wife's MRI is successful. Can you please pay the bill so that we can arrange for the reports?'

I was stunned when I heard the technician's words. I impulsively replied, 'Oh! That's very strange! You hardly got any time with my wife in the machine. She was in and out many times. So, how could you have completed the tests? It normally takes almost an hour! Are you sure about this?'

The technician nodded, looking quite puzzled. He said, 'Sir, I don't know how to explain this. We also could not understand how the tests got completed despite so many interruptions and the patient not spending time in the machine. But when we looked in our systems, we found we had everything we need. So please be assured, the tests are complete.'

I thanked him and asked, 'Sir, can you tell me on first glance if you found anything to worry about in the MRI?' The technician looked at me, smiled and said, 'Sir, there is nothing we could spot. It all seems fine!'

As Chhavi and I walked out of the hospital, I realised the grace that we had just experienced. My heart overflowed with gratitude. What had Babaji just pulled off? How did he manage to complete an elaborate test like an MRI in the blink of an eye? It was overwhelming to experience how deeply Babaji cared for his devotees!

A few weeks later, Chhavi's dizziness began to get better, and after some months, disappeared completely. When Chhavi was ill, she experienced considerable discomfort. Still, on the positive side, this episode made us experience the immortal love and protection of Babaji in the sweetest way possible.

Bobby's Bad Debts

Gurinderjit 'Bobby' Singh is one of my closest friends. We met at the age of ten in Campion School in Colaba,

Mumbai, and have remained best of friends since then. Bobby is the one who introduced me to the internet. Thanks to his inspiration, I became a digital entrepreneur and that helped me transform my life. Bobby became a successful entrepreneur in his field and pioneered the concept of 3D architectural modelling and walkthroughs for the construction industry in India.

Bobby and I often met for breakfast every Saturday morning at the Cricket Club of India (CCI) at Churchgate, Mumbai. We would happily start the weekend discussing our recent work and life events while devouring dosas, uttapams, mushrooms on toast, misal pavs, gallons of coffee and freshly squeezed juices.

One Saturday morning in mid-2017, when we sat down at our usual breakfast table, Bobby didn't appear to be his cheery, happy self. He was withdrawn and glum. I asked him what was bothering him.

Bobby said, 'Alok, the recent demonetisation and the GST tax implemented by the government has been very hard on my business. Most of my customers are large Indian construction groups and builders whose business has suffered greatly. Not only have they put all new projects on standby, but they are going slow on releasing my payments. I sense that some of my less scrupulous clients are using GST and the demonetisation debacle as an excuse not to pay me. Large receivables of mine are badly stuck with these clients, and I am very stressed about it. The worst part is that because they don't need my services at the moment, I don't have any leverage to extract my money from them.'

I understood Bobby's problem and related to it. The Indian business market is terrible when it comes to collecting monies from clients and customers. Everyone likes to do business, but few want to pay. For some perverse reason, many Indian companies, including some of the best-known brands of the country, delay paying their partners and vendors, without assigning any reason whatsoever.

All through breakfast, I could feel Bobby's intense pain and anxiety. I did not speak because I had no solution to offer. How could I remedy an endemic disease that affected all of corporate India? After we had finished, we both walked towards the seaside section of the club with its semi-circular walking path. It was nice to walk a few rounds there and burn the calories we had ingested. As I walked, I kept pondering over Bobby's problems.

Towards the end of our rounds, Bobby tried to make the mood lighter by asking me about my spiritual progress and plans to visit Babaji's cave. Even though Bobby remains positive about my spiritual pursuits, he is a fence-sitter when it comes to learning meditation and accompanying Chhavi and me on our pilgrimages.

The moment Bobby mentioned Babaji, a wave of unknown energy swept through my body. It felt as if an invisible power had seized my thoughts and voice. An unfamiliar aggression overcame me. I stared at Bobby and firmly said, 'Bobby, we must ask Babaji to collect the money for us. Babaji is the master who controls the universe. He can make the most unexpected things happen. Surely, he can help you with your business problems, and so, you must demand that Babaji help!'

Bobby was stunned when he heard my high-pitched voice and noticed my stony gaze. He thought I was possessed. He touched me gently on my shoulder and asked, 'Alok, are you referring to Sri Sri? Do you mean I ask Guruji for help? Or did you say Babaji? I mean how can Babaji help? He is not to be found or seen, right? How can I get Him to help me?'

I was in a state of heightened awareness, and giddy from intense exhilaration. I firmly replied, 'No, Bobby! I meant Babaji. Babaji is omnipresent and omniscient and instantly helps his devotees who remember him with sincerity. I want you to demand help from him...'

Bobby did not ask me any more questions. He remained quiet and contemplative as we walked towards the gate of the club. Bobby probably thought I had become over-emotional about his business problem and was speaking from my heart, not my mind.

When I reflected on my outburst, I knew I was speaking from my heart. I firmly believe that the Gods and Gurus are our guardian angels with whom we must converse without filters or reservations. We must bare our souls to them and surrender at their feet. They know what we need, and what is good for us. All we need to do is ask, and stay assured that they will give us what we deserve.

As we reached the club's main gate, we parted ways and promised to meet the next weekend. I requested my driver to pick me up from the CCI lobby porch. Bobby wanted to stay back for a while at the club.

I was going back home, and the driver headed towards Marine Drive. Just when the car stopped for the red signal at the Marine Plaza intersection, I noticed Bobby calling me on my phone. I instinctively thought that I might have forgotten my wallet or club card, and answered the phone immediately.

Bobby's voice, on the other side, sounded unusual and emotional. I thought I heard him slightly choking. I became nervous and asked him, 'Bobby, what's wrong? What has happened?'

Bobby gasped and said in a broken voice, 'Alok, just as you sat in your car, I checked my phone for messages. I noticed that I had just received an SMS message from my bank informing me that a builder has credited a large outstanding amount of a few lakhs into my bank account. This person was someone who was making all sorts of excuses not to pay me. In my mind, I had written off this money since I had never expected this builder to pay. Now, he has paid off almost all his outstandings. Alok, what is happening? Why did he pay me all of a sudden today? How is this even possible?'

As I heard Bobby narrate the events, tears began rolling down my face. I instantly understood that this was another magical manifestation of Babaji, showering us with His grace and doing the impossible. In a choked voice, I said, 'Bobby, I told you to ask Babaji to help us, and that's what he just did. Babaji is the Mahavatar. He is the King of Kings, the God of Gods, the Guru of Gurus. His ways are beyond human comprehension. The money landing in your bank account was His signal to tell you that He is always with us and that He will come to us when we need Him.'

As I completed my chat with Bobby, I remembered Lahiri Mahasaya's immortal words from *Autobiography of a Yogi*: 'Whenever anyone utters with sincerity the name of Babaji, that devotee attracts an instant spiritual blessing.'

By the grace of Babaji, Bobby and I had just witnessed and experienced this prophecy ourselves.

Connecting the Dots

The great gurus and gods are always with us. Even though some of them may not exist in their body form, their presence is omnipresent. What we need to do is to seek them from our heart and remember them with deep sincerity. These guardian angels protect us and favour us with circumstances that help us overcome our miseries. All the devotee needs to do is to keep his master always in his thoughts.

Exercise

Close your eyes and think of all the people you have been grateful to. Think of your God, Guru or any higher power you have a belief in. Haven't you witnessed their love and protection when you needed it the most? Take this opportunity to thank them and pray to them to always be with you. Try and remember them not just in the time of need but on happy days, too!

KIKO—KNOWLEDGE IN, KNOWLEDGE OUT

In the tech world, the concept of GIGO or Garbage In, Garbage Out is well known. It basically means that whatever you feed into a computer is what comes out. So, if you want accurate results, first enter accurate information.

To live a happy, successful life, I have my own concept of GIGO. I call it KIKO—Knowledge In, Knowledge Out. Simply explained, the more knowledge you have, the more knowledge you use to live your life.

Knowledge, as you probably know, is the hardest to come by. As an example, consider the three solemn vows I took when I was growing up; I was probably fifteen or sixteen years old. Note that I was a pucca South Bombay (SOBO) brat, had a carefree life and thought that the world started and ended at my doorstep.

My three vows were:

1. I will never travel beyond Worli Seaface for anything. (I lived on Peddar Road in South Mumbai.)
2. I will never have an 'arranged marriage', come what may.

3. I will become an investment banker to rival Gordon Gekko from the movie *Wall Street* (the 1987 film).

How did my vows turn out?

1. The moment I stepped out of college and began to work, all my clients, contacts and business dealings happened out of South Mumbai.
2. I had an arranged marriage to a girl from Old Delhi. I am madly in love with her since the past twenty-nine years.
3. I traded drums, supplied water to dockyards, transported steel and machines, made zillions of socks and finally settled down to create online games, but never became an investment banker, leave alone Gordon Gekko.

I chuckle when I tell people that whatever I had sworn never to do in my life, I had to do those things the most. And thank God for that! I cannot imagine how stifling my life would have turned out if my three original vows would have come true. I had limited knowledge about what to expect from life when I was a teenager. I guess that's true for most of us.

An important lesson I have learned is that life never gives you what you want. In fact, life gives you **more** than what you ask for and infinitely beyond what you deserve.

The obvious question therefore is, what should we ask for from life? How do we make a wish list?

If you think about it, it's all about making choices. Often, we believe we are in control of the choices we make, but sometimes, it's the other way around. *Choices choose us.*

And how can we make the correct choices—by using the knowledge and learnings we imbibe as we live. My concept of KIKO has played a critical part for me.

Knowledge is multi-dimensional and cannot be acquired from singular sources. This is where spirituality makes a grand entry. *Spirituality makes you experience knowledge vis-a-vis simply learning it.* Many of the concepts, ideas and knowledge points that have been crucial for my material and emotional success, I have gained from the world of spirituality. It is no wonder that Steve Jobs read *Autobiography of a Yogi* every year. He would have derived something special from that book that his otherwise extraordinary life did not provide him.

My desire to experience unfamiliar ideas and concepts led me to my guru Sri Sri Ravishankar. Observing him, I have learned some of the finest lessons in business, entrepreneurship and conducting my life. This extends to many of my other spiritual dabblings as well. When I visit crowded temples like that of Bankey Bihari, I soak in the energy of the teeming devotees and their unwavering faith in the lord. Each visit reminds me of my humble beginning and the grace Bankey Bihari has showered upon me. How could I have gained my immense luck by living a normal intellectual life?

Stepping Out of the Closet

Almost every other day, I receive messages from people (mostly on Linkedin) that say, 'Alok, I am amazed at how brazenly you share your spiritual stories and pictures with your guru, holy men and the temples and caves you visit. I wonder if you ever think of the negative impact of how people may perceive you professionally and distance themselves from you. To be honest, I love my spiritual side, but I just can't come close to sharing it as publicly as you do.'

In my reply, I write, 'Dear X, let me first answer your question. No, I have no loss of followers, contacts or prestige when I post all the "spiritual" stuff I do. My social media numbers only go up, never down.

'Now, let me offer you a simple, hard-hitting, piece of advice: Don't suffocate yourself. The closet is the most uncomfortable place for a person to live in. Come out of the closet and be yourself.'

In 2015, I was invited to present a content and strategy pitch to a Fortune 500 company based in Bangalore for their startup and entrepreneurship initiative. There were about ten senior people in the large meeting room, listening to me with rapt attention. At the peak of my presentation, I began describing how Art of Living and my guru Sri Sri Ravi Shankar's content strategy could be the best one to emulate for this MNC. I enumerated the reasons and the rationale for the idea. No one in the room flinched while I spoke. In fact, they acknowledged the idea and thought process. I finally won the pitch.

After the meeting, the lady who had organised the meeting came running up to me and took me in a secluded corner. She said, 'Alok, I cannot believe how you referenced Guruji in that meeting with the directors in attendance! I am an Art of Living devotee for the past ten years, and none of my colleagues even know about my association.'

I explained to her that it was silly of her to be living a dual life. The fear of 'what people will say or think' is just a figment of our imagination. No one cares about what you do as long as you get your job done and do it well.

The lady is now an Art of Living teacher, and I hope more public about her spiritual interests!

Regular, consistent practice of meditation and attuning yourself to spiritual teachings allow you to drop all your false pretensions and present yourself the way you are. Trust me, the world loves people who are most comfortable with themselves.

The Art of the Cocktail

Make life one super cocktail. Mix and match everything that works for you into your daily routine. Spiritual practices give you lots of options.

Consider my regular day. In the morning, I devote one hour to yogic asanas and meditation. Immediately afterwards, I go to work and oversee a mobile games company that employs one hundred and fifty people. I play the role of a CEO and manage an extremely demanding and stressful technology business. I am very driven and aggressive at work.

My morning meditation works like a soothing balm that helps me overcome the burnout and fatigue, typical in our industry. Once I go home, I devour global business newspapers and try and read a business book a week. Late at night, I chant 'Om Namah Shivaay' for twenty minutes and go to bed. Meditation provides me with an endless source of energy that renews itself after every session.

Leaping from practicing chakra meditation to data-mining complex analytics, to learning how to hold a rose flower to do Guru Puja or negotiating hard terms with venture capitalists flows seamlessly for me.

I don't separate spirituality, work and personal life from each other. All of them co-exist beautifully for me. *I thrive as a capitalist and as a spiritualist. I am as comfortable in a Himalayan cave as I am in a corporate boardroom.*

My spiritual practice teaches me how to be patient, to think before I speak and to rely on my gut and intuition. When I do business, I learn the importance of making relentless and incessant efforts. That discipline helps me never miss my daily meditations.

My God and Guru give me faith and hope, whereas hard data and facts help me make decisions. Together, things always turn out really well! When I have a complicated tax question, I consult my tax lawyer. When I have a moral dilemma, I ask my guru! Both play an equal and vital role in my life.

I mix and blend spirituality, religion, entrepreneurship and professionalism in just the right proportions to get my life's cocktail right.

What Are the Questions You Ask Yourself?

Growing up is hard. When we come across tricky decisions in our personal and professional life, how can we make the right choices?

Take for instance a young man I met who wanted entrepreneurial advice for his startup. When I asked him what he was planning to do, he replied, 'Alok, I want to set up a factory to produce cheap chewing tobacco for the mass markets and create a great brand for it. Cheap chewing tobacco is missing a great brand.'

I was upset when I heard his pitch and retorted, 'Don't you think you will be producing a toxic product that is known to be cancerous and injurious to those who consume it?'

Instantly the young man retorted, 'But, Sir, if I don't do it, somebody else will.'

'If I don't do it, somebody else will' is a glaring example of being horribly confused in life and making the wrong decisions.

An important aspect of spirituality is the deep contemplation and reflection it evokes. The daily rush of life does not allow us the luxury to evaluate our day-to-day actions and introspect about them. But when you meditate, remain silent for a few hours or days, spend time away from the daily distractions of life, an amazing clarity emerges.

Questions that you may have never thought of, arise:

- What is karma? Do I believe in it? If yes, then shouldn't every action of mine be carefully contemplated?
- What is my real purpose in life? Is it to just eat, drink and be merry or to do something higher? (Many people find this realisation very helpful.)

- Why should I do things that could possibly harm people? Who cares if others are doing it and benefiting?

When I contemplated about my own gaming business, I had a realisation that while making harmless entertaining mobile games was fine, dabbling in gambling games would mean hurting people. A gamble is successful when someone wins money because someone else loses it. This, in my mind, is harmful. My introspection made me decide not to offer any gambling or quasi-gambling games in my mobile games business, even though it presented a thriving, multi-billion-dollar business opportunity. While my investors were disappointed, I persisted. Now, with our existing business doing well, no one has complaints!

I sleep very peacefully at night after taking this critical decision, and have only meditation to thank for it.

Gurus

Do you need a guru? Does the concept agree or disagree with you? Do you think that many of them are fake and out there to exploit people and their vulnerability?

You cannot be blamed for thinking this way.

Having said so, a guru plays a very important role in the upliftment and holistic development of a seeker. The guru-shishya tradition has thrived for centuries now and is responsible for preserving and passing on invaluable knowledge and wisdom of the ages to generations after generations. A true guru and a true student are rare and valuable.

It is said that you do not choose a guru. A guru chooses you.

Personally speaking, I strongly agree with this. I was a spiritual shopper for many years and went to almost every guru I could find, but in the end, my guru found me.

Why does anyone need a guru? There is so much content and knowledge available in the world; what role can a guru play anyway?

It is the same as assuming that with all the books in the world, there is no need for teachers to teach students and hand-hold them all through their formative years.

A true guru does many important tasks. He clarifies arcane knowledge and simplifies it. He understands the needs of a generation and operates in sync with their needs. He creates realistic modules of spiritual practices that can be adopted and easily practised by his devotees. Above all, he is the optimist, the father figure and the fountainhead of happiness and wisdom that makes all problems seem trivial and solvable. This has been my personal experience with my guru Sri Sri for the past twenty years.

A true guru enters a devotee's life after lifetimes of tapasya and deep longing.

If you are unsure, sample a few meditation lessons without committing yourself too much. Make sure you expose yourself to a variety of spiritual leaders. If someone resonates with you and makes you feel extremely comfortable, then you can pursue that guru's teachings a bit more. If you don't feel comfortable, that's absolutely okay too!

Connecting the Dots

Spirituality and meditation are well known sources of deep and profound knowledge. Don't deny yourself life changing, priceless treasures because of your shallow, intellectual ego.

As you live your life, train yourself to be comfortable with yourself! (No kidding.) Drop the false pretensions and be normal. The world will love you even more.

Ask yourself important questions about your own philosophy towards life and the rules you want to live by. Create a unique playbook of life, to live by, for yourself. It's not worth following someone else's playbook.

Exercise

Try out a meditation class. Just like other hobbies or adventures, gift yourself a trial session. You may be pleasantly surprised by the results!

CONNECTING ALL THE DOTS

Towards the end of this book, I want to ask, 'What are miracles?'

Through my experiences, I have learned that miracles are extraordinary events and coincidences that simply happen and are yet hard to explain using the logical mind.

Now, every 'miracle' can be deconstructed through a scientific explanation, but that does not serve any purpose. My intent of writing this book is to understand the subtler principles of miracles and make more of them happen, to help us all! After all, who doesn't want miracles in their lives?

As a revision, consider some of the important principles I have shared in the chapters of this book.

1. To accept situations as they exist in our lives. Personal circumstances may seem painful and unfortunate but could help you in the long run in your life. The idea is to turn negative 'Why me?' into positive 'Oh, wow, me!'

2. Keep a strict watch on the sangat or company you cultivate. Good sangat leads to good things.

3. Some people appear in our life randomly or by chance, but for a specific reason. If we learn to accept them despite their shortcomings, we may learn the lessons that they have come to teach us. It's easy to avoid people, but then we also avoid the messages they carry for us.

4. Prayer is supremely powerful. Even if you don't believe in a God or Guru, pray to the higher power you recognise. Prayers are the secret keys to unlock vast treasures in the world that otherwise remain hidden.

5. The mind gravitates towards negativity. Our focus must be to move it back to positivity. Activities like meditation and exercising help in the process. Try and learn meditation. It is the simplest way to maintain a positive mind.

6. Watch your words. What we wish for usually manifests. If possible, ask for gifts that benefit more people than just yourself. They have a higher possibility of fructifying.

7. Pay attention to coincidences. Some of them hint at a direction you could pursue. People, places and things come together to help you. Try and spot such occurences.

8. Remember that the universe keeps sending us life-changing opportunities and chances. All we have to do is be alert and watchful, and seize the moment when it arrives. And if we miss it, the universe will send us another one soon enough!

9. Seek mentors and guides. People of wisdom can uplift with the simplest of words and instructions. Overcome your arrogance of knowing it all and seek higher knowledge.

10. Share and give. Sharing can give you everlasting happiness. Most sources of joy don't last for long, but when you give, you remain joyous forever. Share what is most precious to you, not what you can quickly give away.

11. Places of worship and meditation have higher energy concentrations. Nature, in itself, is an oasis of positive vibrations. Try and visit such sites so that you can bathe in their uplifting and healing energies.

12. Be unashamed in wishing for things from your God, your Guru or the universe. Ask for what your heart desires. There should be no filters. Then, rest with the belief that what is best for you will be provided to you. Remember the line from the Bible—'Seek and ye shall find'.

13. 'Chanting is half the battle won.' Make chanting a daily practice for twenty minutes a day. Ancient chants have embedded vibrations that get unlocked when you recite them. Take advantage of this knowledge.

14. There are many paths to salvation, and devotion is one of them. Be so utterly and entirely devoted to your God and Guru that they feel compelled to help you overcome your simple desires.

15. Cultivate infinite patience and forbearance. Once

you have mastered these qualities, you will never find anything lacking in your life.

16. Carefully keep a watch on your pride and arrogance. 'Ghamand' (pride) can ruin you if left unchecked.

17. Remember that your God and Guru are always with you. They need not be physically present all the time. All you have to do is keep them in your heart. They will take care of the rest.

18. Practise being comfortable with yourself. Drop the pretensions and veils. The world loves you the way you are.

19. Learn and apply knowledge in everything you do. Remember KIKO!

20. Introspect often and stop living in a closet.

21. If you haven't meditated before, go, try out a session. You will not lose anything, but may gain an experience that could change your life!

Good luck on your journey. May the Gods and Gurus of the universe bless you.

ACKNOWLEDGEMENTS

Campion School—my high school of ten years that taught me everything I needed to know—inculcated in me the art of writing and reading, and gave me some of the most joyous years of my life.

Smt. Savitri Rawat and Shri Damaru Dhar Rawat of Kolkata who introduced Baba of Puri to my grandparents.

The pandas, pujaris, priests, cycle rickshaw operators and halwais of Mathura and Vrindavan who serve Lord Bankey Bihari and us pilgrims.

Gopala Krishna (GK) for being my business guru and helping me set up my first business. Dinu (Dinesh Gopalakrishna) my business partner of twenty years and MK (Mahesh Khambadkone) my partner at Games2win. Both of whom have cooperated with me wholeheartedly.

Sunita Shah, my college friend who introduced me to Art of Living. Sanjiv Sarin, my first Art of Living teacher.

The city of Santa Monica with which I share a deep karmic connection.

Rahul Khanna, my first venture partner in Games2win, who tolerated everything I did, and encouraged me. Bill Elkus and Jim Armstrong of Clearstone Venture, Santa Monica, who have backed and supported me through all the years. Sumant Mandal, my mentor, guru and investor who has encouraged, financed and promoted me through the last thirteen years. Sumant has been one of the most significant contributors to my success.

Nikita Inamdar, my mentor and teacher exemplary of Art of Living.

Deepak Chopra for his infinite wisdom, knowledge, love and compassion.

Daya and Keshava of Anand Sangha, Delhi. They are my teachers, mentors and spiritual guardians. Daya has single-handedly transformed my life so much!

The sincere staff and team of the Woodsvilla Resort of Ranikhet who always take good care of Babaji's devotees. Mahavir—our fantastic guide and a blessed devotee of Babaji—who does a flawless job of organising our trips to the Cave.

Jaina Desai—Sri Sri's international secretary for many years, for her support. Shweta Vyas for her help in organising multiple activities at the Art of Living HQ in Bangalore.

My amazing and forever supportive editor, Karthik Venkatesh, who makes my books shine!

Special thanks to Khushru Irani for being an early reader of this book.

Mr Vijay Poddar of Pondicherry who has been our amazing guide, mentor and friend.

Bhanu Maa (sister of Sri Sri Ravishankar) who has lovingly nurtured all Art of Living devotees and taught us the highest knowledge and spiritual practices.

My loving parents who brought me into this world and let me find my own life.

The gurus and gods of the universe who have blessed me with infinite love and grace. I bow down to you.